Finishing Well

The Fruit of Self-Control

James E. McReynolds
Minister of Joy to the World

Parson's Porch Books

Finishing Well: The Fruit of Self-Control
ISBN: Softcover 978-1-960326-93-5
Copyright © 2024 by James McReynolds

Parson's Porch Books is an imprint of Parson's Porch & Company (PP&C) in Cleveland, Tennessee. PP&C is a self-funded charity which earns money by publishing books of noted authors, representing all genres. Its face and voice is **David Russell Tullock** (dtullock@parsonsporch.com).

Parson's Porch & Company *turns books into bread & milk* by sharing its profits with the poor.

www.parsonsporch.com

Finishing Well

Dedication

Dedicated to Roger Bornemeier

The author's brother-in-law, Roger Martin Bornemeier, stayed in self-control during his 90 years of living in Nebraska. Despite legal blindness, social difficulties, a repaired heart, and so many life limitations. After Roger's mother died, his sister Laurel and I promised his mom that we would move to Nebraska and take care of Roger. Hat faithful promise continued for 25 years until Roger's death. The world might have perceived Roger as the least of these, but now he has received the kingdom of God.

He is one who finished well.

Contents

Foreword

For years now, I have had a gentleman's agreement to write the forewords for my old student and colleague James McReynolds' remarkable books.

I had some misgivings about my own ability to offer a forward to a book on the fruit of self-control. Self-control and patience has never been a problem for me.

When I look back across the years, I cannot remember a single time, from my childhood to old age, when I struggled with this issue. It was simply not a matter that I dealt with.

Maybe it was because I grew up under a volatile father who would have punished me harshly if I acted up at any time. Perhaps it was because I have such a irenic personality that on those few occasions when I needed to become umbrageous over something happening in my vicinity that I just did not have enough taste for combat to even thinking of engaging in it.

One evening when as I was watching one of the daily news problems I usually watch, I was stuck by all the terrible things going on in our world: the dreadful wars in Europe and in the Middle East, Vladimir Putin's scary and unseemly lust for power and dominance, the Chinese penchant for technical supremacy, the escalating violence in our own inner cities and the corresponding arrogance of the gun lobbies at a time when gun control seems to be an impossible dream. In a flash, I realized that these are all convincing evidence of an overwhelming need for self-control everywhere, not just in our individual lives, but in the world at large.

If everybody had only learned to exercise self-control over their own thoughts and actions, we would not be in the mess we are in. People would not have gone to war because they had the impulse to do it or violated their neighbor's territory and personal safety because it seemed to a justifiable thing to do. There would have been a lot more restraint shown on every side. Everybody would have preferred peace and kindness to the sort of problem of madness and mayhem that have become the rule in our society.

So Jim I now apologize for thinking that I had nothing to say on the matter of self-control. I do. I just do not really know what to say or where to say it effectively.

Perhaps I should begin by merely thinking about this subject and praying for its most egregious violators to somehow come to the realization that a world gone mad is not what any of us really want after all. We must amend the situation by exercising more self-control in their realms.

I could single out one or two people that I know who are violating the love-thy-neighbor rule right now and try to think how I could help them to harness their own actions and desires. Maybe I could write an opinion editorial on this problem to be published in the local newspapers.

In fact, I am moved to write a new book myself entitled *Growing Old Is the Hardest Work You Will Ever Do*. I believe that.

These are a few things I could do that might produce positive results in the part of the world closest to myself and help these persons to change everything for the better in our own proximity.

One thing I know for sure, this issue needs to become a big movement in our world today as it has always been for generations past. We must go beyond the desire for more peace and equanimity in our own life environment.

I can sympathize with Roger who died at age 90. I am now 91. I am writing a new book, *Growing Old Is the Hardest Work You Will Ever Do*.
I believe it. It isn't easy. If you don't think so, just wait until you do

it. All life is a struggle, and the gets harder as we age. Our bodies give us lots of trouble. Our minds do not function as well as they once did. Existence in general tends to become more difficult. If we think we had trouble along the way, we just had to reach old age is unbelievably difficult. What we once experienced as child's play compared to what comes later.

My wife Gloria, who is several years younger than I, does most of our driving now. I often just sit at Walmart and watch the stream of people while she does the shopping. Many of the customers keep up needed household duties. Many are older and have great difficulty moving among the cars to get a basket and lean on that while they push around the store itself. How courageous just be out there! I feel guilty that I just sit there watching them as they struggle. It is extremely important that we finishing our course with God. We must let the divine hand shape our final days as it has enabled us to shape our lives along the way.

Life at any age continues to be an enigma to us. This is true in out latter years than at any time in our earthly pilgrimage. If we have ever needed God, it is surely now.

Jim has started something by writing his remarkable book. Now, it is up to us, his readers and publishers, to strive to create a more harmonious and cooperative world. This is the goal for finishing well for individuals and generations now and to come to complete their lives with grace, love, and joy.

John R. Killinger

Warrenton, Virginia

Chapter One
Self-Control

Self-control helps us resist temptation. This last fruit of the Spirit correlates with how we live with the other fruits. The concept of self-control implies that we have a divided self. Each day we produce desires that must be controlled.

"Get hold of yourself. Get yourself under control. Get a grip on yourself." Not having self-control is the experience of our passions running ahead of our inhibitions. Self is the toughest weed growing in our garden of life. We blame others for our problems.

Sanctification is the theological term for becoming fully human. Giving honor and glory to God is the purpose for all life. Finishing well comes with enlightenment of the mind, enlargement of the heart, and the healing of the soul.

The fruit of the Spirit makes us fully human. We are called into everlasting friendship with God. Temperance and fortitude are words used in some translations of the Bible. Fortitude is a temper restrained or the tool for habits of willpower. Temperance is our passion and pleasure controlled but unmitigated. The natural and the supernatural are merged. We cannot become perfectly human until we are partly divine. Our lives become dominated by the Holy Spirit. I John 1:1-4.

The Incarnation is a divine-human encounter. It is the passionate longing of the soul for the love of God. The self is controlled, and life is now ruled by this thirst. Feeling and responding to the overwhelming attraction of God, we know the presence of God.

Grace is the fruit, the gift of divine life. Grace needs a reliable, healthy, and natural ground to take root and bear fruit fully. Delight and spiritual joy keeps us from worldly pleasures.

We do not begin to live once we have solved our problems. We solve problems by living. Jesus spoke about losing your life in order to save it. God desires for us to live a full life with warmest love.

No human is enabled to become full unless there is an emptiness to be filled. We need space to receive spiritual gifts. We receive God's fruit by becoming empty, open, and receptive. Emptiness is not a void or gap, but constructive emptiness. This takes courage and trust. To empty oneself and wait for the filling from Christ.

Self-denial leads to self-mastery. With grace and our personal effort, we help restore balance and harmony. Life means choice and renunciation. Self-mastery means to choose what is human. It is also to renounce what is inhuman. We must not be afraid to love. Unconditional love is not an imperfect, sin-ridden, limited kind of gift.

We cannot use created things for the glory of God unless we are in control of ourselves. We are not in control if we hold onto our desires, appetites, and passions. We cannot give ourselves to God if we do not belong to ourselves.

Self-denial turns over self to the Holy Spirit, so the Spirit helps in our transformation. We end the race as God's masterpiece.

The Fall from grace in when humankind dethroned God and enthroned himself. Humans began to get sick and die. Incurably self-centered, we had no hope of eternal quality of life. The broken bonds of friendship and love. There was no reparation.

The path that leads to eternal life is a narrow one. Luke 13:24. We get some insight of just how difficult it is. Matthew 5:29, 11:12. The concept of self-control is to say no. The difference between worldly self-control and divine self-control. The apostle Paul tells us this is completed in the power of Christ. Romans 8:13, Zechariah 4:6. The power of wrong control comes from the Spirit who lives within us. Titus 2:11-12. The struggle for self-control is a fight of faith through grace. I Timothy 6:12.

Displaying self-control is a matter of responding rather than reacting. Our emotions seize control. We must be guided by reason more than emotions.

Temperance is the English word for self-control in the King James

Version. Self-control is an inward spiritual virtue exhibited outwardly through controlling or restraining our total being including our thoughts, speech, and actions. II Corinthians 10:5.

Solomon used the illustration of strong walls fortifying a city during ancient time. We need to build spiritual walls for protection to live in the joy from the oppressive power of sin.

When humans sin, the temptation is to respond, "I could not help myself." It is our own desires that brings on temptation. James 1:14-15. People sin when they love the objects of our delightful deceitful pleasure more than we love God. Mark 4:19. The idol of our own appetites becomes our authority. When our desires hit center stage, we are declaring that God is not enough. We seek salvation somewhere else.

As our loving Father, boundaries are established for our good. Self-control cannot be a simple "just say no," that leaves ourselves unchanged. Grace is the impetus for self-control. It is the required dynamic. Without God's grace, we will go wrong.

The discipline to say "yes" to God and saying "no" comes from the love and grace of God. Hebrews 12:4. We need to be overwhelmed by the grace of God.

The fruit of this present world shines and sparkles. We are drawn to its pleasures. Early pleasures will fade away. The fruit of self-control and the other fruit will endure into eternal life.

Resisting the influence of the world and our weaknesses causes overcoming sin to be a daunting task. We might make it our goal to be healthier, so you decide to stop drinking sodas and alcoholic drinks. The need to possess and exercise self-control is invaluable to living a Christian life. We must move some things entirely out of our lives.

Restraint comes against constraint. The ability to exercise self-control is restraint. Constraint is a limitation or boundary we build into ourselves in advance. A key to understanding sin is how we structure our lives. Structuring our lives is a skill. Routine practice makes it much easier. Constraint is a powerful tool. We eliminate or at least minimize our time and energy around the things and people who tempt us. We have to think ahead and make solid plans to avoid and to overcome temptations. Proverbs 27:12. Life is filled with potential traps. We might even know what our weaknesses are. Alcoholics might choose to drive home a different way to avoid entering the liquor store.

We might change the people we are social with. If our current friends are involved with sinful and harmful practices, we will be pressured to join in with these sinful activities. Saying "no" is much easier to say to an illicit relationship. We should not get involved with that relationship.

Holy Scripture teaches us to examine ourselves. We must look for sin and focus on repenting. Lamentations 3:40, I Corinthians 11:28, II Corinthians 13:5. Constraint as well as restraint are necessary. Reflection is a mystery. It does not come entirely from ourselves. Self-control is not about bringing ourselves under our own control, but under the power of Christ.

The fruit of self-control comes from speeding time and energy with God. II Timothy 1:7. We are never alone in our journey to live God's way. God will help us to know what we must work on.

Approach God in prayer with an honest attitude. Get back up and try again. Get a grip. Get a life.

Paul puts it another way in Romans 7:23. Paul is describing the pull of human nature. Natural is part of this world. I John 2:15-17. Self-control is required to show love, not as the world does, but how Christ loves.

Imagine a small child throwing a tantrum. She throws her toys and acts out of control. Twenty or thirty years later, this same adult person is yelling in her boss's ear for making her rewrite a report.
Balancing our God-given gift of free will involves doing what we might want to do with doing was the right thing. We choose to allow the Holy Spirit to be in control. Romans 7:21-25.

16

God shows self-control by patience toward the children of God when we struggle. Longsuffering enables God to give second, third, or unlimited chances with love, mercy, and grace. I Timothy 1:16. To have eternal joy during difficult circumstances, we must make peace. I Peter 1:18. To be patient with other people, to bear with them, and to be gentle in service to Christ will help us show compassion and mercy. II Timothy 2:24.

Jesus displayed the fruit of self-control. He was patience with the disciples, even when they showed their unbelief. Matthew 6:26, 17:20. Revealing himself to the sinful Samaritan woman at the well. John 4. Jesus showed self-control during his earthly life.

Jesus knew what he was sent to earth to do. He demonstrated self-control in submitting to the Father's perfect plan. II Timothy 1:7. With the Holy Spirit living with us, we possess self-control and demonstrate the fruit of the Spirit. So we live in the strength of the joy of the Lord. The purpose of the Incarnation was to begin on earth the kind of life God lives eternally. Christ is our only access to the Father. Christ is the Living Bridge between God and us.

Being guided by the Spirit rather than being controlled by our natural sinful nature is the point of Ephesians 5:7. A self-controlled person works in moderation, not excess. Emotional swings and extreme behaviors are not the portrait of self-control. I Timothy 3:3. A believer can act like Christ, regardless of circumstances. Romans 13:14.

God loves us. This loves is expanded to include all people. Friends delight in one another. They find what love means transformation. The only response to divine love is an irrevocable commitment. Friendship with Jesus is unique and wonderful friendship. Christ is like us. The difference is that Jesus infinitely perfect. He was down to earth and yet God of heaven and earth.

Christ delights in our company. He loves us with everlasting love. That love has transformed our love. It is no longer a self-indulgent, narrow, or cramped. In him, dreams become reality. Christ is the brightness of the glory of God. If we were to write down all the significant data about Christ, John tells the world could not contain the books that must be written.

Children loved him. Anyone who found themselves in trouble would run to him. He was strong and virile. He arose early in the morning to pray. He often spent whole nights praying. He traveled on foot. Sometimes he had no time to eat. He lived life zestfully. He knew what his mission was.

The poor were his delight. He had concern for little things. Nothing escaped his love and care. We admire historical figures, but nobody falls in love with them. It is not possible to know Christ without falling in love with him. Jesus' era was one of love.

We can realize that Jesus brief life was finished well. His farewell address bears the ineffable marks of his divinity.

He had such an amazing, instantaneous effect on his chosen disciples. He was like the potter with his clay. Christ now dwells within us. He is closer to us than we are to ourselves. He is more real than we are. He fills our souls with a riot of joy.

The apostle Paul relates exercising self-control through training his body to live before God so that we will not be disqualified from preaching the joyful Good News. I Corinthians 9:27.

Paul warns the Galatian believers about having run a good race, but then stumbling. Galatians 5-7. Through self-control we persevere and endure conditioning and to continue to run so they continue to be finishing well. Acts 20:24.

We supplement faith with the knowledge of God to lead us to self-control. II Peter 2:5-8. Paul says we must renew our minds every day, Romans 12:2. We continue to focus on Jesus Christ and growing the fruit of the Spirit.

When we stray back into sin, we can be forgiven. I John 1:9. We are to remain joyful I Peter 4:13, Philippians 4:4 in all our circumstances. The fruit of the Spirit grows and matures as we are transformed in Christ's image.

Every human being who is being continually saved by faith has the seed planted inside to glorify God and to be more like Jesus. The fruit is one fruit with many characteristics. It grows integrated with every part together grafted into the Body of Christ.

Finishing well means differing things such as ending life with an easy retirement. To die a pain-free death would be the desire of most people.

Finishing well means to follow Christ to the end of our earthly journey, completing the will of God, and hearing the phrase "well-done, good and faithful servant."

The fruit of self-control begins with love and grace is where finishing well starts. As John Newton wrote, "Tis grace hath brought me safe thus far, and grace will lead me home."

A Christ-centered life knows that there is no greater joy than to know God in Christ. They focus more on loving Christ than avoiding sins. Christ Jesus is the spring from which flows in every spiritual fruit. Hebrews 12:2.

Finishing well means knowing the purpose of our life journey. Their calling is to glorify, serve, and love God. Philippians 3:13. To be focused is to eliminate things that are unnecessary. Hebrews 12:1. Grace and discipline are spiritual friends.

We have an old self and a new self. These compete and dominate our lives. Self-control is absolutely the most effective fruit we have to sanctify ourselves. Christian freedom expresses itself in self-control. Psalm 40:3.

Some things are easily seen as out of control. If we cannot go to sleep, we try to adjust. We might get up and have a cup of sleepy-time tea. We will eventually fall asleep. We cannot control when the sun rises.

We are not in control of our circumstances. We have had no control of who are parents or the members of our family. Most people have no control over their governments. We choose to lead healthy lives, but nobody chooses the length.

A teachable spirit with a humble foundation. Finishing life's race means we are to be lifelong learners. Paul the apostle was teachable until the end. II Timothy 4:13.

Finishing well means having a network of supporting relationships. These are our mentors and those who pray for us. Self-control happens over a lifetime. The second half of life is when we experience a new conversion. We mature in differing ways to discover that self-control is actually a surrender.

Most of the it occurs in our second half of life. It is a process of getting to know our selves, acceptance. God created us in the divine image. Our uniqueness and individuality. Like God, we have a relationship with all creation. To be a human, we unfold our uniqueness, and we fully experience who we are. This comes in the second half of our spiritual journey.

Our earliest self-concept stays with us as joy or pain the remaining years of life. The rebirth process is a miracle of moments when one freely chooses to live, to accept life, to be human as we accept our human condition. We experience the tensions and paradoxes. No longer can we strive for perfection. We accept that we can never attain such a status. We become aware of the sinfulness of others because we have encountered it within ourselves. The person we became in the first half of life is not in commend.

Those unconscious depths within us will be discovered. We call this "a change of life." God loves us with full knowledge and acceptance. The Lord is calling us to go beyond who we are in our present image of ourselves.

Accepting ourselves as humans is to accept the power for good and evil that is within us. Dickens wrote about Scrooge who was led to see the evil within himself. He had a rebirth, and he began to experience goodness from within. He enjoyed full access to his innermost self. He could no longer deny the ugly side of his life.

Like Scrooge, the Spirit enables us to accept where things are in the world where we live. We become like children. The second half of life fills us with questions. In the first half, we assumed we had answers.

We touch the surface of who we are. We become aware of a kind of evolution. We realize the need for balance in our lives. We begin to resolve the conflicts of the polarities of life. This process is natural. It is a journey that leads us to maturity, integration, and wholeness.

We will never be a truly finished product. The first half of life, we struggle to build a strong identity. This is a radical transformation. It is the opportunity to become more than we are. The call of Christ is, Come follow me." Come and commit yourself to new insights, to a deeper depth. Come and respond to the Spirit within yourself. Come and grow in the consciousness of awareness. Come to love and trust yourself and all its parts both conscious and unconscious, he known and the unknown. Our unconscious is the womb for a new birth and new insight. Forgotten ideas have not ceased to exist. These are still present. These can rise again spontaneously after years of oblivion. The unconscious is composed of our impulses, perceptions, intuitions, urges, thoughts, inductions, conclusions, and feelings. Our unconscious is reality beyond the rational.

The fruit of self-control involves all these factors. God begins everything. We cannot begin to strive for our goals unless God takes the initiative. We live with boredom and the ordinariness of life. We live empty and joyless lives. There is hope.

Those with faith in Christ should become a sparkling and ebullient kind of person. We should radiate the glory of Christ. In our age of despair, it is time to hope, to share it, preach it, write about it and pray about it. Our despair is not despair of God. Hope in what God can make of human beings can come out of despair.

Hope is the supernatural force that is within us. It is created in our soul. Hope is the fruit of a regeneration of our Savior. It is beyond human reach.

Life is too short to choose what is second best, or not our best self. If that is not within our range, we become uninspiring people. The Holy Spirit keeps the fires of enthusiasm burning. If we stop being like children, we stop being ourselves. Heaven begins on earth to the extent we are striving to get into a life of self-control.

We are given eternal life. This life is in our present and in our future. We experience full joy now and in our expectation. If we desire God, we get the characteristics of God. We share in God's divinity, knowledge, love, and life because of our sincere desire.

We have the privilege to lean on God and expect everything with mercy. We cannot count on individual effort. We strive in the body of Christ. We are supported by a community.

Our friendship with Christ enables us to dare as Christ has overcome the world. Our longing for heaven does not be the reason we think we are not responsible to the world. We are restless and alert. Every improvement of life and each attempt to increase beauty and fruitfulness comes from us showing the fruit of the Spirit. Hebrews 1:11-12.

We have been created out of love and grace. Each one of us is the complete and total object of the love of God. If God would stop loving me, even for a brief moment, I would no more be.

Whatever has happened during my lifetime has been planned from all eternity by God because of love. If we bind ourselves to this reality, we will be enthusiastic, always in control in every situation. John 3:26. This is the epiphany of God. Our Creator is burning and glowing. Jesus lived his life on earth so captivating lovable causing humans to turn themselves around. We become whole, and we fix our will on God forever.

We learn to love God by thinking like God, acting like God, and being transformed into the image. We learn to love God by loving God. We prove by our deeds that we prefer God to anything else. Intimate prayer helps God fill the whole self and not only the soul. The whole person is touched. The will to love becomes actual love. Every relationship which has been transformed by Christ glorifies God. Ephesians 1:9-10.

Christ had to enter our personal situation to create a new relationship with God. Christ forged a new link between God and us. There is now a totally new response to the Spirit. Human life was meant to be a response to the love of God. We say, "I live now, not I, but Christ lives within me." John 14:6.

Praying to Christ means entering into our relationship with God. In prayer we implore God to reveal divine presence with simple and loving attention. The pinnacle of all human achievements is union with God.

Wit infinite zeal this is God's will. We respond to God's friendship with prayer. The impulse that us to pray is the awareness of the indwelling God in the deepest paces of our souls.

Prayer has been called a spiritual echo. It serves as an alertness to reality. Prayer prepares us to live and also to die. The big decisions of life are made long before the crucial incidents in our moments of prayer.

Everything that happens finds expression in prayer. Praying people become more sensitive and more inventive. Life attempts to deceive us by being more than it appears. We meditate upon the eternal and timeless reality of God.

Life is more than breathing in and breathing out. Life is our self-experience and our self-realization which is important in the fruit of self-control.

Praying causes us to be aware of the miracles of life. A miracle is a "sign" from God.

Chapter Two
Acceptance

In our time of finishing well, we must accept the limitations that come as we grow older. Time passes. Culture changes. Acceptance of age requires living in the present, even if the past has been rich in unforgettable experiences.

The enforced inaction of retirement can bring on an early death. My wife enjoys flowers. The flowers from her brother's recent funeral will remain fresh and alive for a few days, but soon wilt and fade away.

Time passes. We cannot preserve flowers from the past. Life is like that.

Acceptance of growing older is to live in the present. If we are alive, God still has something for us to do. Joy and inner strength, satisfaction in our work, and acceptance contain more influence than heredity, our diet, and anything else. Spiritual strength transforms us with the zeal, the energy, and joy.

We are helpless at our birth and at our death. Lent emphasizes he reminder, "You are dust and to dust you shall return. II Corinthians 6:8-10. Remember that you are. God's Dust. (James Hillman, *Blue Fire*, p. 22)

One of the Scriptures I read at every funeral is Psalm 23. John Killinger offered an engaging sermon on this Psalm of David. In a time when Killinger felt he would die. He wrote: "I went to bed that night. I went to sleep at first. Then I woke up in the stillness of this house and thought about dying. I was going to leave it all—my wife, my children, my home, my work, everything. Leave it. Maybe with a few months' time." (John Killinger, "The Overflowing Cup," *Pulpit Digest*, p. 17)

We all must accept the fact of our death. We all live with death as we grow older. Death draws nearer. The closer it comes; we begin to want to finish well.

There is a table set before us as our cups are overflowing. However, we continue to stay empty. Adultery is the only means of satisfaction. Filling our cup with a sudden blaze of passionate love turns ordered existence into inner turmoil. If we "fall" in love with a manipulative woman is the cause behind the mad things lovers do.

If her target is an older man, she'll delight in making him feel thirty years younger. She has transformed his life. There has been introduced into his soul, mind, and body more than he has ever experienced.

In our unhappiness, we accept a fear of the vanity of life. We are born. We live. We choose our actions. We suffer. We die. We hold our craving for a feeling of really living, of fulfilling an instinctive aspiration. Every love affair brings a specific pleasure. Lovers and even married people believe they have chosen the ideal partner for satisfying the instinctive urge.

Many marriages fail in a dull existence. Couples refuse to face the conflicts of mutual adaptation. Every encounter and every relationship becomes more complicated. There are also unforeseen traps. We must be continually renewed. If that never happens, people continue indefinitely preparing for life instead of living it.

There is a certain truth of the mind among those who accept their lives. Acceptance is the attitude of living our real lives with conviction. Premature acceptance is an apparent acceptance that confuses our minds.

God so loves all people. Psychotherapy is one means of grace that enables me to understand individual difficulties and all the obstacles that come as we journey on the path of faith and faithfulness.

We are sensitive to criticism. We become anxious to succeed. Often, when counseling others I am filled with remorse if I been able to help some person.

I pray that God may use my writing of books to be a way for some unknown reader to find joy in times of trouble. I share real-life stories of myself and others. The stories are of sweeping enthusiasm as well as disappointment. Some become stifled, irritated, and humiliated at each tale of failure.

To fully understand life is to understand God. The infinite joy in the scriptural perspective is that it changes our attitude toward the events in our lives. They reveal the purposes of God. Philippians 1:12-14, Romans 8:28.

Listen to God. Be guided. Life is a journey. It is directed and made possible by God. I enjoy traveling to renew life at home and to expand myself. My precious brother-in-law Roger had no liking for long travels. He was happy in his Nebraska surroundings. This is where he always lived. He shared that most of his joys were from living on the farm. Even in his home, things that disturbed his routine irritated him. He never wanted his home to be changed in appearance.

Some places retained a significant importance such as Roger's bus trips to see the special places in Nebraska. At age 90, he told and re-told the same stories. He was always waiting at his garage door for somebody to take him to eat at the senior center or to travel with me to worship at my pastorates. When I would appear, he jumped for joy, the joy of going in the car with me.

I believe that Roger will feel more joy than the rest of us as he lives in his heavenly home, the Next Place. I Corinthians 7:29-31.

What will Roger's eternal resurrection be like? This is a glorious mystery. I Corinthians 13:12. His journey will be a personal journey. Roger will have a personal fellowship with God. He is no longer blind in sight, unable to walk, living a lonely life. Roger will inherit his full share of everything God will provide. There will be no handicaps or diseases, and as the Bible tells us, he will be "revived."

Our earthly journey involves our whole life. It is worthwhile. With God, we can put our whole heart into whatever we do. God is not to be left out. We must open our eyes. Think new thoughts.

Risk more. Be willing to change your ways. This is not an easy task. It is difficult to find what he will of God is. Isaiah 55:8.

We must accept that only we can choose aspects of how we spend our time. We are in control of the things we think about. I control my daily habits. We control how we spend our money.

The only thing we can absolutely control despite our circumstances is what we think and say. Nobody can force this on us.

A common malady is that many will not accept their own bodies. It becomes an obsession. I knew a woman who had her nose repaired so she could be more satisfied with her face. People don't like their thick legs, their height or being too tall, being too fat, or having an unpleasant voice. Friends try to assure them that they are handsome or beautiful.

Their worry Is maintained by beauty products, movies, literature, and magazines. Acceptance of our physical bodies means to stop comparing oneself with others.

Acceptance is knowing our unique gifts that are unparallel. To be human is to unfold the uniqueness of who we are. We have a complete understanding of the talents and skills we bring to the world.

We believe that we are good, and we are unconscious of our motivations. Our heads are in the clouds. We are not aware that our feet are in the clay. With awareness and acceptance of this truth is a test of our courage. Being truly human we come to the point that when we look out from our prison windows, we see the mud as well as the stars.

Accept that every person on earth has a crack in themselves. This is true solidarity, and this realization is redeeming and humbling. Accept that each person's human weakness is a strength. Our inner environment—our true authentic self-graces us with full acceptance. In this full acceptance is where miracles happen. The person we were in the first half of life is no longer in control. The self that we were called to be in the first half of our lives is that unique individual that each person is, slowly emerges with our self-control. This realization and commitment is the entry door to the second half of life.

Faith leans on our full acceptance of the Word of God. God speaks. We accept the Word and then we respond. To accept in faith is believing in the power of the resurrection and the life of Christ. He rescues us from our false self.

The Word was made flesh. Here is the single instance in the history of humanity when one person was caught up fully in divine life. His life has been prolonged and extended. Scripture says that we can only begin to worship God but in faith and faithfulness. We accept and discover an intimate union with God. That is the ultimate reality.

Accepting all the aspects of our salvation does not mean we lose our freedom. At the end of the race, He is ruled and directed by love alone. Faith is an act and an attitude. It is seeing everything in light of eternity. Faith helps us to see ourselves as cradled by God's personal love. We become rooted in God. We live progressively in the Spirit.

Salvation is dynamic, not static. During every day of our lives, if we are generous to God and faithful to grace, God infuses into our soul knowledge of all things needed. With faith there is only light shining within us.

Spiritual disciplines include prayer, study, and fellowship. These are means to an ending well in intimacy with Christ. Without self-control, fidelity in spiritual discipline declines and decays.

Our purpose is to grow in Christ. "I have decided to follow Jesus. No turning back." The joy of bearing spiritual fruit builds our confidence. God is never indifferent to us. God uses suffering for our good as we are united to God in Christ. Faith increases our capacity to trust in God through the times we do not understand divine purposes.

Those who finish well in any era and generation have an ongoing learning and ability for humble acceptance of things not seen and not yet.

Faithfulness and growing hope transcends and endures. Winning the life race cannot be possible without the caring support of others.

Believers who finish well do things for the good of all people. In times such as the Great Depression, people squandered the resources, gifts, experiences, and hard-earned insights. Those with power no longer invested in the lives of their fellow humans.

Ending life well is to be able to say with the apostle Paul, "I have fought the good life. I have finished the course. I have kept the faith." Second Timothy 4:7.

"The joy of the Lord strengthens us" as we "run the race that is set before us." Hebrews 12:1.

Chapter Three

Work

The joy of work involves doing each moment what is unique.

Nobody else will be who I am. No other moment in time will be the same as the present one. Every action, each success, all experiences shows us what living in the image of God is about. God permits us to be cooperative in divine work.

Work is as much about passion and joy with the assurance that we are in the correct place. Love of God becomes our purpose. It is what we were born to be. I Corinthians 12:4-7.

The joy of work integrates human values and economic success. Fun at work involves fairness, social responsibility, and integrity.

Sometimes it is best for us to stay put. Decide what's next and best for you. If the negative feelings are related to your work, changing jobs makes sense. If these feelings are not related to work, changing jobs will not help. Evaluate your calling or chosen career and plan the net move to determine what is the right path for you.

If you cannot move up or find no joy in your work, perhaps you need to move out. Depending upon your skills and credentials, almost any available job should be open to you now.

Our human culture has made an idol of work. Work, in reality was created by God before the Fall caused by pride and sin. Genesis 2:15. Before the Fall, work was joy. Work is the expression of the journey of life.

Ending well was not even imagined when our ancestors who lived from 1930-45. At the end of 1929, industrial production declined. Businesses failed. The Great Depression was an unhappy time of falling incomes and rising unemployment. Product prices dropped. The whole international economy suffered. Depression was the word and the psychological and mental health as assets shrank. Few people used the railroads, so railroad workers were desperate as nobody went anywhere. My mother had never been ten miles from her home since her birth. People who have lived before and since cannot imagine how horrible life was. Everybody was forced to fight the fight for subsistence.

A majority of Americans and nearly all foreigners believed that he Stock Market crash of 1929 caused the Great Depression. The world suggested that the United States birth this worldwide disaster. In years before, economic difficulty went through periodic difficulties that were self-generating. The Industrial Revolution and forms of capitalism brought periods of growth and prosperity, as well as years of stagnation and decline. There were climate shifts such as the Dust Bowl, wars, demographic trends, and epidemics of disease altered economic conditions in dramatic fashion. People in the United States made it worse by withdrawing their savings from the banks and the declining Stock Market.

Scripture, especially Proverbs praises work and warns against idleness. The biblical viewpoint praises the skills of weavers, goldsmiths, vinedressers. Exodus 31:3-5.Being forced to become idle with no work was a spiritual problem. Herbert Hoover's presidential administration did nothing to help. People turned to religion for hope and inspiration.

Jesus worked as a carpenter. Mark 6:3. Paul worked with hands making tents. Acts 20:34. Scripture speaks of the "hands" of God. Isaiah 45:12. God in Jesus works always. John 5:17.

People live their entire lives within the limits of narrow specializations. People work honestly in their personal interests, never questioning themselves of things differing as competence alone is not all there is to work. Work is the secular and spiritual united together. Faith and faithfulness come within our work, not outside of it. Married women did not work in paying jobs. School teachers lost their jobs if they married during the Great Depression.

Our time on earth is a gift from God. It is renewed in every moment. Time itself belongs to God. Making up for lost time is not possible. God never asks us to do more than one thing at a time. Scripture uses the word *Kairo,* which means the moments of God. We must work not only in what and when God wills, but to do it when God wills in divine time. Now I am writing in our hard times. Wealth is not a sign of a life well-lived. Mario Puzo said that behind every great fortune was a crime. That's another way to look at it.

Doing life in God's way brings the feeling of joy in what we are doing in each moment. We will never experience the same moment.

When I was writing the first pages of this work, I was watching snow falling in my cozy office. Now my tying is running more easily. Before starting this book, I read several books. I brought to my mind all kinds of ideas on this subject of the fruit of self-control and my conception of its importance in my life. Today, I don't want to stop.

It was easy to take the plunge. The difficult part is to keep at it, so it ends well. Writing a book is like playing a game of chess. There is the risk of losing. Equally, hopefully we might win. Life is a game that is played only once. Every choice. Every move. Every initiative. These determine the game. My grandson Ethan likes the use of a time clock that limits the time allowed to decide what he will do with his chess men. When he was a child I could beat him, but not today. He is an excellent student at Lafayette College in Pennsylvania.

I became perplexed as I began the composition. One-page written calls for doing another one. I myself am in control of my own time and effort. Self-control is my lifeline.

When I was asked to preach on my platinum jubilee, my 70 years in ministry, the congregations congratulated me on my accomplishments. Suddenly, I felt it was all pointless. I have plunged into so many places and so many times and differing ways for my communication of my personal story.

I have hesitated and wondered if I can risk and take action. I have at times been unable to resist the urge to commit to myself to doing another thing. Many of my projects have not been given the light of day.

What if I die and not finish well? The instinct of trying to control my life is like the instinct of death haunting the mind of every human who now exists on earth. We want to make a personal mark which will survive us. Ending well is to love well. Eternal love is rare.

Our work survives to give us joy and a legacy of for those we love. We are willing to accept every sacrifice. Self-control and our choice to serve is a divine gift. It is a sign of the fruit of love. When we realize the holy quality in our instincts during our brief life journey, we feel responsibility towards God to direct our travels according to the will and control of God.

Joy! When we achieve a graduate degree, the accomplishment in a moment life, the world, and other problems appear to fade away. Of course all of us have a natural fear of failure. Fear is there, but so is joy. President Franklin Roosevelt said the only thing to fear is fear itself. His administration did something. The football stadium in Bristol, Tennessee was built during the depression.

The last mystery of our existence is knowing how to conduct ourselves well. We must depend on the sovereignty of God. Every experience of fruitful love and fellowship points to self-fulfillment.

Appearance of self-fulfillment is not fulfilling. Appearance of humility cancels humility. The appearance of love is not real love. The appearance of faith and faithfulness is nil if we do not live it with commitment and conviction.

We are given one life to live. We have no control over which years we will exist. Every minute of our existence is filled with choices that are vitally important. Life is truly a huge game. Death hangs on every human life. To hold back death is delaying the moment when our final balance will be drawn up. At death, the Book of Life will be closed. I Corinthians 15:26.

Death is a transition into a new and joyful life. Revelation 21:4. In light of the resurrection, death is not a failure. We call the slow journey to death old age. Old age brings progressive weakening.

Death is rarely lucid, serene, and fully accepted. When Jesus was presented to the old man Simeon, he accepted his death. Luke 2:29-30.

Our life journeys are a game. We must learn to play it. A person who lacks self-control is destined to failure after failure. Life on earth will always be difficult. Patience and endurance (long suffering) helps us achieve self-control.

To finish life well we need not dream of a different life. We must live it under God. The path of the life journey is composed with failure. During my travels and preaching joy in Scandinavia, I observed that Finland and Norway are poor nations. Sweden and Denmark are rich nations. The countries are located close to each other. All life is difficult wherever our earthly place of existence might be.

The biblical perspective changes our attitude toward the events of life. Philippians 1:12-14. This reversal in our attitude gives us the strength and complete independence, or self-control. Romans 8:28.

Our task is to listen to God, to permit ourselves to be guided, to accept the life to which the Spirit calls us. Birth and death are big parts of life. From start to finish God teaches us patience for self-control. Kierkegaard wrote, "What I really lack is to be clear in my mind what I am to do. The goal is to understand myself, to see what God wishes me to do to find a truth which is true to myself, to find the idea for which I can live and die." (Soren Kierkegaard, *The Journals*, p. 15)

My definition of work success is to perceive a loss of track of time when I am preaching, teaching, or writing. I want to finish well and be remembered for making a difference in others' lives.

Some people die after their retirement. Others keep on doing what they have been doing, but they are losing their joy and enthusiasm. I am looking for ways to make a contribution. That is how I see finishing well.

When I served as pastor of the Faith Baptist Church in Nebraska City, actor Jack Nicholas came to town to film the movie "About Schmitt." It was about a man who gave his life to his work. The company gave him a gold watch and told him to come by for a visit anytime.

When he drove to the office a few days after his retirement, the people were too busy to see him. I played a bit part in the movie. I was with others walking down the street in front of the office. That was it. It was about as exciting as the theme of the significance of work.

Work is a problem. Many people do not have work. Unemployed adults. Poor people. Youth. Children. Older people. For some, work is their only source of self-esteem and the meaning of life.

Somebody in the middle stage of life (perhaps 25-50) with no work is a much graver situation than a person at the same age who enjoys work.

We say that all people are equal and should enjoy inalienable rights to life, liberty and the pursuit of happiness.

The modern life of a person or country demands a multitude of known and unknown tasks to create a lifestyle of harmony and human life. Humanization of work is badly needed. A person's right to work, to enter things that contribute to the world should be a human right or need.

Our generation is full of those who are deprived of the joy of working in something they are suited for, and which meets the needs of those for whom we work.

The second half of life is a call to transform ourselves so that we finish well. We begin to have a felt sense for things other than what has been our primary concern. There is a lack of wholeness, joyfulness, spontaneity, and expansiveness.

It is wonderful to acquire a job you enjoy. Jobs do not made life perfect. Some say, "Without my job, I will never be a complete person." Therefore, the prime source for happiness becomes a source for unhappiness.

Nothing that happens to us has a negative or positive value unless we assign the value. Encounters and events overwhelm us.Dr. Norman Vincent Peale, the father of the power of positive thinking, told us that the worst events of life can bring something positive. Peale would agree that the positive in life is not apparent.

We do own the power to see challenges or failures as the best thing that ever happen to you. Focus your eyes on the bright side. That describes your valley of hope.

"It ain't over until it's over" was one of the wise sayings of Yogi Berra, Hall of Fame catcher for the New York Yankees. Finishing well accepts that truth.

Nobody knows what the future holds. We realize that today is full of challenges. These will continue for the rest of your life. What joy it is to be in self-control.

Those who finish the human race will experience in their later years a new strength, enormous power, and wisdom.

During each season of our life cycle, we are called to a new dimension of becoming in areas of physical, emotional, relational, and spiritual growth.

Our images of ourselves changes us as we experience a movement within us. Self-control is yielding to a kind of magic, to enact and pre-empt the future. Our minds are being prepared to accept the incredible and the unimagined, to enter a world of freedom. We are now allowing the child to be born in us.

Chapter Four
No

One of the powerful truths that Jesus shared in his preaching was "Let your yes be yes, and your no be no." Jesus had only three years to complete his mission. He had to say no to many things. After Jesus was baptized, he went out in the desert wilderness for 40 days. Companionship, food, and water were not in the hot area.

It is a miracle we realize as we cannot even endure fasting for a few days. God is calling us to endure whatever comes.

This book is for all ages, not just those who are planning the end of their lives. Teenagers and young adults find it difficult to say "no." It is easier to go along than to let peers pressure you to do what you do not desire to do. Teens feel that if one does not go along, others will laugh at you or refuse to be friends.

During the Reagan administration, you were told just to say "no." This may have worked for some who were determined and strong. During the years that I spoke to millions of students in local public schools, I talked about children and youth to share a reason something is a bad idea. I wrote two books on methods of prevention for school groups K-12, and another for churches. Young people were taught self-control in making excuses of why one cannot and stick to it. They could suggest a differing activity, So there will be an "out" for those who take you up on it.

My task and purpose was to open young minds to a vision. The vision was to structure the atmosphere and culture that youth breathe. High school and college students are easy to inspire. Their world is one of wonder. They are eager to explore.

Youth can keep repeating themselves. Sticking to your decision stops the persuasiveness for doing something you need not do. Young people can talk to their closest friends about how they feel. Then there is support for each other. There is power in numbers. We must be taught that we will never please everyone. If there are those who cut their ties with you, let them go. We can lead by our intuition. Some have more effective intuition than others do. Intuition is our best radar system. Gut feelings enable us to think about what we want before we express it. Authenticity rather than likeability must be the focus. I know this takes courage.

We must sacrifice that part of us that wants to please others. Perceptions are really miscalculations. We say "no" with grace as a way of respecting our own time and space.

Children and youth in the public schools ask about what words they can use. Possibilities are, "Let me think about it first." Or say, "Now is not a good time as I am busy with other priorities right now." Your intuition will enable you to say the most effective words. Courage leads us not to spread ourselves too thin.

Saying no is an exercise in mindfulness. Address others with respect. That gentleness and kindness gives us the awareness of the power of saying "no." The overwhelming joy will bring good things into your life now and you will finish well in life to come. Life is too short to not feel your best.

We want our young people to be accepted, to get along, to learn how to make money, to share our comfortable existence. We forget to teach them who they are and where they are going. So our children are rootless. They are prey to every potential leader including gangs. We drive them to become rebels without cause.

We need self-control because temptations are all around us. Our world is filled with temptation. Not every temptation results in sin, but these become benign diversions. If left unchecked that become unhealthy indulgence or addictions.

Self-gratification is dangled before us promising an easier path. Self-control helps us say yes to the more difficult path to what God created us to be. Those sins we fight against are the fruit of an undisciplined life.

An uncontrolled tongue produces gossip. Lust comes in an

uncontrolled mind. Undisciplined anger comes with pride. Be the master of your soul. I Corinthians 6:12.

Christ has called us to self-control. Mark 8:34. The words of Paul offer help. I Corinthians 9:24-27. Growing as a Christian requires self-control.

Self-control is the ability to create a protective wall that prevents us from giving in to the desires of the flesh. With self-control, we will be able to say "no" to things that will harm us or others.

Self-control makes a big difference in our life journey. We cannot control every circumstance in life, we can control how we respond to each situation.

Cultivating self-control is difficult. Each person has differing sins that she or he struggles with. Taking time and energy to discover self-control enables us to avoid things that destroy spiritual, mental and physical health.

After the Fall, we have struggled with sin the differing ways. We do not overcome sin by the work of God in our lives. The Holy Spirit helps us. Galatians 5:16-18. Self-control is the fruit of the Spirit. Galatians 5:22-23.

Each of the fruit is crucial in finishing well. God wants us to live in conformity to the ways and thoughts from God. The Spirit helps us as we pray and exercise self-control. II Timothy 1:7. We will come to love what is good. II Timothy 1:8. These verses are talking about requirements for an elder in the church. It applies to all of us.

By living upright, holy, disciplined and self-controlled lives we will be more like Christ and bring glory to God. There are dangers in not having self-control. Proverbs 25:28.

The apostle Peter encourages us. II Peter 1:4-7. Falling prey to the corruption, deception, and temptations of the world puts us at high risk of developing sinful habits. These result in misery, pain, and weakened relationship with God.

Because God loves us, there is forgiveness and receives us back. The Holy Spirit will again teach us self-control. Joseph in the Old Testament demonstrated self-control. He was the son of Jacob. He was sold into Egyptian slavery by his own brothers.

His character caused his days to be filled with joy. Potiphar was Joseph's master. He put Joseph in charge of his entire household. Joseph the slave made life good for Potiphar.

Joseph was a handsome man. The wife of Potiphar noticed Joseph and became infatuated. She found a moment when she could be alone with Joseph. She dressed in her sexiest clothes, and told Joseph, "Come to bed with me."

Joseph refused her offer. Joseph said, "No. I will not sin against God, and I won't violate my master's trust."

She continued to seduce him. One day she grabbed his body. Joseph fled away from her. Sexual trouble comes uninvited, knocking on his door. Joseph resists.

She is charming and manipulative and her side of the story lands Joseph in jail. Joseph had self-control. He did not show anger or shame. I John 5:4.

Saying no is never easy. It always has a cost and consequences that we never could anticipate. There is a disassociation of fantasy and reality which is difficult for our realizing that we must say no.

The practical consequences of not saying no come from our choice, our own decision. Neurotics know themselves quite well. Thy are even afraid of what they know, but they have no self-control concerning their self- delusions. Of course, they continue to do actions that are wrong. They are tossed about by their uncertainties.

Without self-control there occurs more disasters. The uncontrolled hold spontaneity, social ability, and simplicity.

These qualities cause saying "a profound no" less likely.

We might think that we have made a mess of our lives. Now it's too late to say "yes" to healing. That old thought is like giving up in a basketball game at halftime. The best team usually wins even if they are 20 points behind at the half. The faster we change our ways, the more years we finish well through our remaining years.

Recovery is the time to catch up. When I served as chaplain and counselor at Valley Hope Treatment Centers in Lincoln and Omaha, I did many assessments and talked with many young people. It is to their advantage to start. Getting help now, every life opportunity will still be there. You will be able to go to college. You can start a family. You can work toward a career. With new skills and self-discipline, you can do more than you ever imagined.

Take care of yourself. Shower or bathe regularly. Keep your hair well groomed. Brush your teeth and floss. Watch what you eat. Avoid junk food and foods with less sugar. Exercise feels good and adds to your health.

My therapy work at Valley Hope consisted of helping addicts find goals in life. We helped them to express what they wanted out of life. Saying yes is to accept that life is not always fair. We could just fold up and remain miserable. Or we can say "yes" to a whole new and interesting life.

It isn't what fate does to you that's important in the essence. It's what we do with our fate. Self-control begins when we put our shoes on. Self-control appears as an impossible dream. Set long and short-term goals. Nothing worthwhile can be accomplished in a day.

I always addressed per pressure and the importance of self-control. Think ahead to situations that often happen. Plan what to do in each encounter. When you say your "no," speak firmly. Show confidence. Troublemakers will keep their distance. Whatever you do, don't let other of your peers make decisions that affect your life. You are put in charge of your health and life.

The fog will lift. The uncontrolled anger, depression, resentment, embarrassment, and pride will slowly diminish. That me-first, selfishness will be less of a problem. Reality is much easier to face and accept. Evaluate the harmful past actions. Bad things happen to the best people. Humans can survive almost anything.

Nobody is ever expected to be perfect. Progress is the key. Look back and see and enjoy the progress.

When we work with those with no self-control, crisis management is needed. Human clients lose their jobs. They lose out with love, and they are stressed beyond their limits. Sometimes our life journey is a bowl of cherries. At other times, life is the pits.

All of our substance abuse clients are required to do a fearless and honest moral inventory. Most addicts have done this activity several times.

This may be the right time to make amends for all the hurtful things done to others. We must forgive and forget. Focus on relationship healing. Relationships change. They grow slowly.

The word "intercourse" refers to both verbal and physical communication. To communicate we must engage and touch each other. Even poor communication will help. Much is lost in translation of the message.

The body speaks. Body language is powerful. Language of our limbs express what a person is thinking or feeling better than our words. There is a danger of jumping to the wrong conclusion. Criticism is not always personal. Being in self-control is to evaluate each situation. Be careful not to just show unhealthy anger. Saying "no" or "yes" requires one to be assertive. Being passive or aggressive. Some will not express feelings and they become angry and resentful.

Assertive is being clear and making a point without offense or hurt. Calming assertiveness is the answer to joyful living.

People will never agree on everything. Successful living requires deep respect. Beware of the expectation of a negative reaction. We must be prepared to lead people in their decisions in a way that is alive, sincere, fresh and effective.

Lack of self-control is a dimension of teaching that we have neglected. We have deprived our youth of the freedom to be themselves, their very best selves, the opportunity for each one of them to develop to the highest power.

Self-controlled people make their "yes" a firm yes, and their "no" a firm no.

Chapter Five
Maturity

The gateway to Christian maturity is discipline. Discipline is not an innate quality. Discipline is cultivated. It is a steady determination to keep on keeping on, choosing to do what is required to be done. To do what we want is our tendency. Life is bound up in movement. It is to continue to maturity as the goal, "he pressing toward the mark," as the apostle Paul has written. The last end of anyone is union with God.

Only in the days of our ending the race of life can we understand what we did not know in most of our life beginnings.

Contemplation is an experiential and loving way of obtaining maturity. John 17:3. Mature Christians find joy and peace. John 17:22-23. Grace is the cause of that inner life. Lifelessness is lovelessness. Anything that impedes or hampers love weakness life.

Christianity is the fire of Christ to light in our hearts and in the world. Maturity is necessary before we can serve. Immature people concentrate on their own development. Perfection is the maturity of the supernatural life.

One perfect or mature Christian glorifies God more than thousands of immature ones. Mature people have established roots in the Spirit. Job 34:14-15. All reality has its deepest meaning in the reality of God. Rootlessness leads to ruthlessness. Immature people have severed roots.

To become uprooted from the Spirit is to be unhinged. The immature will dry up, stagnate, with no zest for life.

When an undisciplined child does not get what she or he wants, they throw a temper-tantrum. Adults also throw fits. They cannot contain their emotions. I Corinthians 13:11. In our thinking, we must be more mature. I Corinthians 14:20.

A person is mature at any age if the person is open to growing. The moment we close the door or take a position of passivity, immaturity takes over. Becoming an adult means one is economically independent. Sexually active. Eligible to vote in elections. Legally accountable. Independent of people who raised you. We have uneasiness with these definitions. Childhood can be a model for adulthood. To be an adult we must maintain the ability to have a playful attitude toward life.

Self-control issues stem from immaturity. Maturity is to become fully developed to control emotions, thoughts, and desires. Self-control is "temperance" in the King James Version of scripture. Other synonyms are sound mind and discipline Proverbs 25:28. We hold ourselves in bondage to unseen controls. James 1:14-15. James is saying that we must rule our desires and set boundaries to protect our vulnerable souls against temptation.

With the truths of God, the boundaries help us to not give into our desires. These with problems of losing our tempers means to give up control over others. Healing involves pruning. John 15:1-2. Childish ways of thinking need to be pruned and removed from our minds.

After the Spirit has pruned our childish thinking, we rely on Jesus for strength and righteousness. We can draw from Christ's divine power to produce spiritual fruit. We become divine partakers of the divine nature of Jesus. Only then can we rule of desires with self-control. II Peter 1:3-8.

Discipline is training to help us mature and exhibit self-control. This not easy and often brings pain and suffering. Hebrews 12:10.

A little boy lost a footrace in his elementary school. He was angry when he got home. He was quite jealous of the other kids who won that race ahead of him. The lad's father saw his son's bad attitude. He told him, "Son, anybody can be kind when they win. That's really easy. But when you lose, and you are still kind to the winners, then you are on your way to becoming a mature person."
Taking hold of the means of God's grace ignites spiritual flourishing. According to Titus 1:5-9, maturity means to not be open to insubordination or debauchery, not be drunkards, or quick

tempered. Christian leaders must be self-controlled, holy, upright, disciplined.

These are the marks of qualified elders. The Holy Spirit is our source for self-control. Galatians 5:22-24. The Spirit lives within us enabling us to produce these fruit. Romans 8:9.

Self-discipline is needed to experience consistent results. The goal of parenting our children is to raise mature children.

A self-control person has normal human passions. And most pursue whatever they desire, so they become impatient, ungrateful, and demanding. Brilliant people make foolish choices. Some never learn from their mistakes. If we taught to say "no," our perspective is not skewed by our passions.

Self-control is being a responsible person who accepts accountability for personal actions. Others are not blamed, and no excuses are made. A responsible one is faithful in work habits. This reliability and integrity are possible as our passions are no longer in charge. We often develop a victim mentality and someone else is to blame

The goal of finishing well includes self-control, responsibility, and wisdom. Self-control goes contrary to our human flesh. We desire to control others, or our circumstances, and that brings conflict. James 4:12. We are to allow the Holy Spirit to continue the sanctifying work within us. II Peter 7:5-10.

A mature person takes ownership and responsibility. This takes self-honesty and acceptance. If life keeps going wrong, the mature one looks inside for answers as to what actions contribute to the situation. The mature know that they don't know everything. They never argue to just be right. Open minds, open eyes, and open ears look for opportunities to learn something. They say, "How can I learn and grow from this?"

Those who reach maturity gain a level of self-understanding with regard to their behaviors. They decide how to approach situations to reach successful resolutions to problems. We feel discouragement. So we think about quitting. We will not recover if we quit.

If we really want to love more and you do not have self-control, you will not do it. Without self-control, we will never become generous. If we wait until we are in the mood, we won't move. If we do not accept that truth, we will never be able to have any self-discipline. We will end up destroyed and with no influence for God.

As we mature as Christ's followers, we will continue to struggle for self-discipline. Procrastination and impulsiveness will derail us. We must embrace our dissatisfactions. God's will is to make something beautiful in us.

Becoming fully mature is always a work in progress. Not everyone will become enabled to act successfully and maturely in each situation. The goal is to have a clear mind as they rationally dictate how to be effective. They can perceive all the available options to find a successful resolution.

Beware of good intentions. We must bring our intentions to completion. Keep working out your salvation. Create new habits. As we grow older, we sit on the floor after getting up to pray, we have the all-inclusive struggle to care for our bodies. I once went to a chiropractor, wo kept various sayings on his office walls. One said, "So when you wear out this body, where are you going to live." We must run with endurance and not become weary. Figure out what God wants us to do. God will give us a special grace.

They hold no false sense of self that is ego-based. They believe in their own ability to use patience and effort to deal with whatever comes their way. Staying resilient in the midst of setbacks, upsets, or disappointments, they acknowledge their feelings, identify the possible solutions, and take steps to move forward. We will grow in self-control as we allow the Spirit to subdue our desires.

Outside of Christ, we have no self-control. Self-control keeps us alert. I Thessalonians 5:6-8. It stirs us to remain faithful and to pray. I Peter 4:7. It is our protection from being easily swayed with a weak will. II Timothy 3:6. Self-control prepares us for action so that we are not ineffective and unproductive in the kingdom of God. I Peter 11:13-16. We gain self-control when we give God control in the power of the Holy Spirit.

The fruit of the Spirit is a clear picture of Jesus who perfectly reflects the character and nature of God. Jesus reflected self-control in his life on earth. Hebrews 4:15. Jesus was tempted in every way, yet he lived without sin.

Temptation tries to win us over through our sinful nature. James 1:13-15. The Spirit gives us new goals for finishing well. Galatians 5:16-18. God's Holy Spirit lives inside us. Without self-control, Temptation wins out every time. Romans 8:5-7. Without self-control we destroy a legacy we have been building for years. We can do his in just one day. We bring a powerful threat to those heroic works we have completed. Lack of self-control undermines everything.

A sound mind comes as we mature. I know I have come to understand that a sound mind is fundamental to the enjoyment of life. Without a sound mind and self-control, we are destined to bring destruction upon ourselves and upon the purposes of God. We will remain defeated by all kinds of circumstances. Without a sound mind, we are invaded by things that cause us to become unstable in our convictions. Being self-controlled is the foundation for living a life of selflessness and righteousness that reflects Jesus and gives glory to God. Only with self-control do we have the power to bring our sin under control.

Sin wants to grow. Whenever we give sin a doorway, it is not satisfied to being a little secret. Sin destroys whatever it inhabits. John 10:10.

Lack of self-control destroys a marriage, relationships, a career, and finally life itself. Proverbs 16:32. Self-control is a requirement for achieving healthy goals such as being debt-free, having healthy relationships, and a rich and rewarding calling.

Scripture tells us that self-control is not only the ability to impose restrictions and boundaries upon ourselves to achieve goals to the glory of God. Self-control results from the Holy Spirit in our lives. Self-control keeps us grounded in a sound mind.

Self-control dictates the pleasures of our flesh, instead of being controlled by them. We are habitual beings. We live better if we have established healthy habits. Habits empower and benefit well-being.

They inspire our development.

Bad habits take away our time, health, growth and keep us from the life that God intended for each of us. Our bodies thrive on perpetual habits. Habits control us instead of giving us control. Serious and strict measures are required to gaining back self-control. Without them, we are powerless to the desires of our bodies. Our human bodies respond to our habits and not to good intentions.

Old habits must be replaced by new habits. Habits come from our spiritual convictions. These convictions are turned into habits. Our willingness to suffer temporary pain, be inconvenienced and delay instant gratification brings the joy in our spirits. Romans 6:10.

Self-discipline leads to being like Christ. I Corinthians 9:27. Hebrews 12:10-11. Physical exercise is hard and painful, but necessary for righteous living and sound minds. A sound mind is a correct judgment about the things that are based on the Word of God. Sound minds embrace the perspective of God. Sound minds does not come naturally. The world tosses many obstacles in our paths. John 16:33.

God gives us a sound mind. It is up to us to keep it. II Timothy 1:7. The word sound-mind from this verse is interpreted as self-control, self-discipline, and good and sound judgment. This is the apostle Paul's encouragement to younger Timothy to not be intimidated. A sound mind does not happen to us by default. We must renew our minds. Romans 12:2.

I always pray before giving a sermon, sometimes vocally," Let the words of my mouth and the meditation of my heart be acceptable in your sight." A sound mind is a gift from God. Never surrender it to a circumstance or life-situation. Galatians 5:16.

May God help us gain back control of our minds. This is the reason Jesus directed us not to merely watch, but "watch and pray." Pray without ceasing. Praying is meeting Christ. To prayer is to know God by experience rather than by hearsay. To pray is to stand before the real Christ. Praying is sitting child-like to listen to the God who "alone has everlasting life." That is the hope that we will finish well by showing our faithfulness to God.

Chapter Six
Eternity

Finishing well is to keep the endless reaches of immortal life in our hearts. It is startling to think how swiftly few are our years before we will all be under the daisies.

Living with an eternal perspective is to fully realize that God is eternal. Psalm 93:2. God is not limited by time. Revelation 22:13. God existed before time. God exists now and will continue to be when time passes away.

Living in the here and now requires courage. Life is a series of moments called now. The past has no power over us. Permit your soul to steady itself. Contemplate the days ahead. These days are to be welcomed and fully accepted. Each moment is a human adventure to be enjoyed. This eternal joy brings contentment and a positive sense to life.

Time is for the benefit of humanity. God delays the coming of the end of this world. II Peter 3:9. The sense of timeliness is not understood from our human perspective. God understands time and how much we have left to respond and find the eternal remedies during the short time we will live on this earth.

God created us to live for eternity. Ecclesiastes 3:11. That is the prime reason for our walk with God. Ephesians 5:15-16. Love covers a multitude of sins. I Peter 4:7-8. We are required to walk with wisdom, praying to our eternal God, and loving all people we encounter. Our priorities and actions are directed by the Holy Spirit. If we are serving the living God. We find eternal joy and comfort. When we talk about Jesus, we must live what we talk. II Thessalonians 1:10, John 11:25. God confirms our faithfulness. Our behavior reflects our confident belief in eternity. Having this perspective is to life a Christ-following life. II Corinthians 4:18.

The Spirit helps us realize eternal life in visions to open our eyes and to see what is at stake. Suddenly we know the present life is really a brief life and a brief window for our opportunity to invest in things that will last forever.

Eternity is the image of an endless horizon as far as we can see as a heavenly realm. Eternity is a complex idea of how we understand God and our place in the universe. Eternity defines the qualities of God. Genesis 21:33, Isaiah 40:28. We use eternity to understand the timeframe of our future existence. John 3:16.

Concepts of eternity are rooted in how we perceive time. It relates to God's interaction with time. The Psalm writers depict God living an innumerable number of days. Psalm 88:29, 90:2. God's life is contrasted with our brief lives. Psalm 39:5, 90:3-10, 103:15-17, 144:4. Scripture also shows God apart from creation and outside of time. Genesis 1:1-5, Ecclesiastes 3:11, Isaiah 43:13, Romans 1:20.

The New Testament affords Jesus a divine temporality as a key part of his divinity. John 1:1, 8:58. The culmination of the New Covenant comes through right belief is eternal life. John 3:16. Our Old Testament says the covenant is eternal as God is eternal. Proverbs 8:22-31, Isaiah 9:6, Micah 5:2, II Corinthians 5:1, Revelation 21.

Those who wrote Scripture were not able to understand or touch eternity. They could only grasp it in their imaginations. When Jesus spoke about heaven and heavenly things, the crowds did not understand his meaning. John 3:12.

Finishing the race, we have the hope of eternity. Human flesh cannot endure without dying. Eschatological details are not known. Things along life's journey are temporal for they do not stay real long enough for us to see, but things not seen are eternal.

Finishing well means taking a long view of living, to look at things with the end in mind. The urgent things crowd out the important. We must adjust priorities in eternity's light. This will give us an enlarged perspective.

The whole idea of forever comes into my mind, and I think of ways and means and words to comprehend it. I wonder what an eternal heaven could be like.

It appears ridiculous to attempt to teach about heaven. The fact is eternity is outside human understanding. We just cannot fully understand it. Eternity is as long as we can imagine added to infinity.

Theologians have attempted to communicate eternity as an endless or immeasurable time, our state after death, the state of being in infinite time. We might more easily grasp what could last forever into the future because we understand the thought of something coming into being that did not previously exist. In reality, we do not have any authentic understanding of what future actually is. We say it is a long time into the future beyond what we know to be the longest time we can conceive.

We try to picture in our mind that something or someone has always existed. Something that has never been created. Think of God as a starting point, and never had a beginning.

The average human would need more than 30 years to count to a billion if he or she counted for 24 hours every single day. A trillion is one thousand billion. We would need to keep counting for 30,000 years non-stop.

God has existed for one trillion times one trillion times a trillion four times repeated number of years.

In light of eternity, which amount of time that God has existed is but a fraction of a second. Eternity also has a future. It would be easier for us as we do not have to deal with the idea that there was never a starting point. We are trapped in the framework of time.

It is important to think about these things, if for no other reason, to increase our anticipation and gratitude towards God for giving the gift of eternal life. When Holy Scripture speaks of eternity, it means life or death. This helps us to become clear about what is eternal.

God is eternal past and future. Humankind and angels are eternal future. The present state of the universe is not past eternal nor future eternal. God has never changed. Hebrews 1:10-12.

Those who have accepted God's gift of eternal life through love and grace on God's terms, will spend eternity with God. Jude 21.

Trying to understand eternity helps us to become excited and appreciative of eternal life. Time is something God created as part of the reality that we know, leaving God outside time. Being outside of time completely, God is not bound by time. God exists apart from time as we understand it. God is equally present in all points of time in our existence. God exists in fullness at all times, in all places, and in all ways.

God has always been in both the past and the present and the future. God is already in the future. In finishing well, the idea of eternity is important to think about as it gives us hope and joy when we understand what eternity in heaven means.

Even if you were to life for 100 years or more, it will seem like a whisper, a vapor, a blink of an eye compared to eternity.

In the beginning Scripture places humankind in the Garden of Eden. It was such a peaceful, joy-filled place. It was a place of perfection where there is no anxiety or pain and suffering. It was God's eternal place.

People are forever looking for a place. II Chronicles 6:18, 21. Faithfulness often involves localizing God to a certain place. The children of God focus on an eternal place.

God's eternal purpose is the salvation of humankind. God appears to certain persons in certain places such as Jesus speaking to Paul on the road to Damascus. When the time was ripe, God came to earth in the human form of Jesus. Philippians 2:5-7. To be in the likeness of women and men is to be bound to places. Jesus needed a birthplace, and God chose a stable in Bethlehem. The four gospels tell of Jesus' earthly ministry, of particular encounters in clearly defined places, leading to Golgotha. Matthew 27:33.

God gave us Eden trusting us to care for it. We were given responsibility. John wrote of eternity in Revelation. He used the

language of incarnation as Paul had spoken of the resurrection of the body. I Corinthians 15:35-44. Writing about the heavenly Jerusalem coming down from heaven at the end of time.
Revelation 21:2. It is a certain place that he is describing, which has walls with dimensions the angels measure with trees of life in that city. Revelation 22:2.

This eternal place is where there will no longer be death, or mourning, or crying out in pain. Revelation 21:4.

The hope of heaven is a clear and present reality for the followers of Jesus. What we do in our earthly journey is important. If we are recognized for our efforts, that's certainly joyous. The Next Life is what matters, when our work will be recognized by God.

Eternity matters. There is more to life than in the here and now. We are always a work in progress. Our calling and our life purpose is exciting. Rewarding. Exhilarating. Working through our worst experiences generates joy. Life challenges are no reason to quit. God will give you strength to the end and beyond. Resting on our laurels is unthinkable. Life is a miracle that is too valuable to waste.

There is no joy listening to the sound of a rocking chair while we wait until the undertaker comes to our door. I want this book to inspire you to keep on. Cherish each day with joy and anticipation. God gives us the strength to give insight and truth to those who are bent on creating havoc and disharmony. In the end, the Lamb wins.

We are getting older. Nobody lasts forever on this earth. Enjoy each moment. Keep your passion aflame. The secret to finishing well is doing excellent work, being with good people, and receiving and giving love.

Most people do not finish well. Physical decline. Arthritis. Aching bodies. Financial hardships. Death of friends and family. Loss of purpose. Most do not want to deal honestly with old age. We live longer years, but our culture makes us feel obsolete much sooner.

Finishing well is continuing continuity between what you do before you retire and what you do afterward. We must not become useless. A wise therapist once told me, "Jim, it is important to recognize that we can retire from our jobs, but we can never retire from our calling."

Finishing well means keeping our sense of responsibility. Encountering and engaging the world will make each day a day of joy. That, to me, is the Christian view. The world's view tells us we are over the hill as we reach a certain age.

Home is the waiting room for heaven. The hope and joy of heaven comes with our faith and faithfulness. Heaven is not just a vague concept for those finishing well.

In many and differing ways believers demonstrate that life goes from success to significance. Our words and examples of living life for others remains long after we live here.

If you were at the end of your life, looking back at where you are now, what would have happen to you to feel good personally and professionally about your life?

You would get under the agenda of God and out from your own plans. We are to surrender to something greater than ourselves. We are surrendering to a vision quest that is better than keeping on trying to do it all our way.

I think most of us would rather live a shorter life that is fun of vital ministry than just to rust out. There is more to life than temporary security.

We look for models of folks who finish well. It is our challenge to discover the essence of what's important. We dare not keep on doing the things we have tried before now.

Knowing the present world will end, we make every effort to be spotless. I Peter 3:11-14. As we realize our coming citizenship in heaven, be become responsible citizens of earth. Laying up treasures for eternity, we give time, money, and talent.

Little choices become tremendously important. Our actions are empowered by the Spirit are of eternal consequence. God and the Word of God lasts forever. Our earthly lives need not be wasted. In small and unnoticed ways, we invest this life in eternity. Today's faithfulness will forever pay rich rewards. An eternal perspective changes our actions and our attitudes. Living with eternity in our minds infuses us with joy and purpose that sustains us. If we believe we are going to live forever in a kingdom with God, we will experience joy.

Our eternal salvation helps us fix our eyes Jesus, not on the popular culture. This is what we mean by the term "eyes of faith."

This involves risk. We must go against the grain. We need to suddenly grasp a new feeling of urgency. Life is really uncertain. We take our last breath not when we desire it. We think our next breath will be there in the next day.

Our goal is not just to live so many years. It's not even to become prosperous. We are to make a meaningful life out of an ordinary one. Self-controlled people have an enduring sense of something that is deeper than our emotional responses. We seek deep and enduring delight in what is the most significant goals of life. Remember, life is too brief to not feel your best.

Living with eternity is the most wise way to live. This eternal perspective keeps us from useless dreams and material gratification. We will not waste our time chasing temporal things.

The most important experience is to know that we have been born again and again. John 3:3. This is the path where we please God. When we accept by faith with Gid's love and grace the death and resurrection of Jesus the Christ, the Spirit moves into our spirits, and we are adopted into God's forever family. Romans 8:15-17.

We gain eternal perspective as e are filled by the Holy Spirit. Acts 4:31, Ephesians 5:18.The Spirit never stops working in our lives. Being filled with the Holy Spirit is to become fully yielded to God.

Sinful self-gratification, focus on lusts of the flesh cannot be continued with the eternal perspective. We must store up treasures in heaven. Matthew 6:19-21. We store treasures in heaven with things we do for Christ and his glory. Jesus told us that giving a cup of cold water is cause for reward.

Sending time in the Word of God as is possible. Psalm 119:11. We continue to need to be refueled. Romans 12:1-2. Just as our automobile needs more than one fill-up with gasoline, we need regular "washing" of the Word. Ephesians 5:26.

To gain this eternal perspective we must stay conscious of the truth that this world is not all there is. Each day counts toward our final journey. The Spirit teaches us, and we receive minds that focus on the Bible. In my own writing I deliberately cite passages that are not so much a part of me, I cite their authority. Colossians 3:1-3.

Keeping an eternal perspective is not just a natural thing to do. The Spirit redirects our thoughts toward the eternal views.

Chapter Seven
Prayer

Our sinful urges are part of our lives because that is our nature. We can turn to God in prayer to get help in controlling our impulses. Most view prayer as a monologue. They do all the talking. They announce to God their own desires. They do not wait for an answer. Effective prayer comes from remaining silent in the presence Habakkuk 2:20. We are not to pray in another worthy manner. Prayer is a means to become firm in this world. Prayer is a trusting and attentive attitude. Prayer is a whole person activity. Praying is transcending everything but moving all of it. We are open to timelessness s we pray.

We can get control of the words we speak. We often blurt out words that hurt and offend. The Holy Spirit will guide us. Otherwise, we flow with useless drifting with every current. Order and self-control come with prayer. God is able to speak to us at any time and in any place. We will not be timid, hasty, or feel unloved in any way. Silence becomes painful with confusing thoughts. Prayer is a way to bring in God constantly. Prayer is a way to experience the world. We are unrestrictedly falling in love. Prayer is a whole person surrender. When this incarnating of God is affirmed, prayer is happening.

In all Christian history prayer has been a journey inward. Prayer opens consciousness beyond itself. Our cry for God we move beyond our closed egos. Prayer breaks the division between the conscious and unconscious.

Prayer is the most important tool for changes our situations and circumstances. Blessings will come with a strong and consistent prayer life. We will gain self-control by maintaining peace in our hearts. Isaiah 26:3-4. Prayer puts us in touch with reality. The awareness of this reality s beyond the distortions of self-interest.

Prayer is a vision of an interrelatedness to all that exists. During the afternoon of life, one believes that one must work as if everything depended on oneself and to pray as if everything depended on God.

With a new intimacy with God, we are now leaving the familiar to enter encounters with the unfamiliar.

Remaining in the same job and keeping the same relationships will not hinder our radical change. We see things differently. There is a shift in values.

The unconsciousness of the womb was the place where we knew unity is approached again. Now we can approach God in prayer with that same sense of unity and completeness.

We become passionately concerned for the poor. We are forgiving and we have renewed compassion. (Donald Gray, "Prayer: Passing Over and Coming Back," *Worship*, pp. 300-301)

Prayer is coming out into the open. We come to God just as we are. Real prayer allows no pretense. God loves us unconditionally. With God we can finish our life race with assurance and joy.

Remember the old Wednesday night prayer meetings? For at least an hour we were expected to close our eyes without falling asleep. We were to focus our attention on God. Sometimes it was a silent conversation. During my teenage years, my prayers lacked structure. They were far from eloquent phrases sprinkled with Bible verses. Something seemed off when some church leader repeated the same prayer every time. Luke 17:9-14.

Our pastor preached on the Lord's Prayer from Luke 11:1. Jesus had completed his prayer. He and his disciples were prayer together. They wanted to say powerful things as Jesus did. Eager to become like Jesus, they asked if he teach them how to pray.

They were sincere in wanting to communicate with God in prayer. They realized that they needed guidance.

Prayer may be simple. It is just talking with God. Prayer is a learned skill. Time, work, and practice are required. Every day the disciple spend most of their time with Jesus.

Compare this so-called the Lord's Prayer in Luke to the same prayer in Matthew 6 in the Sermon on the Mount. The words are similar, but not exactly the same.

Laura Bailey gave some ideas on how to draw nearer to God in prayer. We can acknowledge God's glory, Bow before the Lord in humble adoration. Thank God for divine provision including grace and love that sustains us through eternity. We confess and repent of sins, believing one will receive forgiveness and we will forgive others for sins against us. We pray to become like Jesus.

Prayer is personal. It is a privilege. We can pray any time. God is more concerned with the attitude of our hearts, minds, and souls than our actual words. Life is complicated. Prayer is not so.

The Holy Spirit prays on our behalf. Romans 8:26.

Prayer gives us wisdom and direction to enables us to make good choices. Proverbs 16:3, John 16:13, James 1:5. Only then will we observe doors opening that humans have no power to close. Matthew 7:7-8. Prayer puts us in the right place at the right time. Wherever that is, prayer helps us to remain strong during trials and temptations. Prayer helps to renew our strength. Isaiah 40:2831.

Intimate prayer helps God bring to our surface wrong attitudes so we can release them. Prayer talks out and expresses our concerns. Nobody can love us like God does. An intimate and fulfilling relationship with God results from prayer.

Prayer is crucial to seeing all that God has planned for our lives come to pass. God's plan involves taking steps of faith that require supernatural provisions. God has a unique plan for our lives. It begins when we surrender to Christ. Nothing we could imagine could be better. Ephesians 2:10, 3:20. John 15:16.

To fully embrace all God has planned for us requires bold prayer. I Peter 5:8-9. I pray as I write and flip through my Bible to be incited for my writing. It is really not complicating, nor is it unusual.

The character of God is reflected in ways and thoughts that are supernatural. To keep control of ourselves, we surrender everything to God.

Prayer causes God to intervene on our behalf. Jesus emphasized the importance of prayer. Luke 10:38-42. Our prayers must be in line with the will of God. I John 5:14-15.

We are ambassadors in our place on earth. We minister and heal people in Jesus' name. When we pray, we pray in faith. That will help us to realize miracles in our lives. When we pray, we simply believe that our prayer is already answered. Mark 11:22-24. Intimate prayer brings us the wisdom of God. As the promises God has made in the Word, we build up our faith and active faithfulness to believe. Romans 10:17.

We are all children seeking our joy path. We are called to fulfill a mission which we do not know how to do. The angels and the Spirit guide us without our own realization. We are guided step by step.We look back to the way our life journey turns. He know and feel without human knowledge that God has been mysteriously guided us. We could never do anything just by ourselves. We confess our inability to see what God wants for us.

We pray that God will give us "daily bread." Self-control involves discipline in eating. We choose what we eat and how much. Gluttony is a sin. Self-control is a fruit of the Spirit. We are directed to eat healthy food and avoid foods that harm our bodies.

Food and drink are essentials to live. God tells us watch what we drink. Alcohol becomes addictive. Being drunk is a sin, so we are to be filled with the Spirit.

Gambling ruins our finances and robs us of our relationships. A common means for gambling in the United States is sports events. College basketball teams have faced "the death penalty," which means not being allowed to play for a year or more. Pray that the Spirit will help us to avoid places and people that push us into the harmful habit.

Self-control is needed for us to keep calm and composed. We cannot be ruled by anger. Not controlling our temper is a city without walls. Rage and being irritated is fought with forgiveness and long-suffering.

Controlling lust is to bring our passions under the Spirit's guidance. Compulsive sexual behavior is called hypersexuality or sexual addiction. Sexual fantasies, urges, or behaviors get an intense focus. Engaging in masturbation, multiple sex partners, use of pornography or paying for sexual pleasure. There is no self-control.

Uncontrolled lust damages relationships, lowers self-esteem, health, and career. With the Holy Spirit, one can learn to manage compulsive lust.

Sexuality is a God-given energy that creates life and selfless joy in the life of another. Sexuality is rooted in the deep human need for others. Sexuality is a natural and human force. This overcomes separation to enhance life. This separation begins at birth. The search for completion and union accompanies every human until we die.

Sexuality is such a powerful energy; it brings ecstatic joy. Out of control sexuality brings human suffering. For this reason, mature sexuality is essential to healthy Christian spirituality and finishing well.

The human drive for friendship, communion, joy, delight, immortality, family, wholeness, and transcendence. Sexuality is good and essential for the human journey. It focuses on the encounter with another person with the physical expression of desire and love.

Human intimacy involves closeness and the ability to bond with another person. Intimate friendships are warm and affectionate ways between mature adults who show mutual love and support.

Experiences has taught us that those who engage in sexual misconduct are impoverished in intimacy with others, self, and God.

The restlessness in our searching drives us outward to bring satisfaction for our incompleteness by doing more activity, distraction, or entertainment.

We must accept our strengths and weakness. We need not become anxious about our sexual feelings, our desires and attractions. Depending on our age and human development, sexual impulses will be troubling. Desire for passionate genital expression can be controlled.

Intimate prayer brings inside God who grows each of the fruit. Self-control is a gift of the grace of God, so ask God to develop self-control in you. Titus 2:1-12. Be encouraged. Self-control is available.

The fruit of the Spirit begins with love and ends with self-control. Love comes first because it is the first fruit which contains all the others. Self-control is required, but it means nothing without love. Prayer is the means that we will grow more like Jesus with self-control.

Self-control is like a war between our impulses and doing what's right. Ecclesiastes 7:9. We find no help in unhealthy coping mechanisms.

Prayer and meditation are powerful healthy ways to enable us to focus as we give our concerns to God. Philippians 4:6. Keep in mind that one mistake in self-control will not be the reason to give up. When we make mistakes, we can see it as another learning opportunity. Self-control is a life-long journey.

Prayer helps us to figure out what God wants us to do. Listen. We are just too noisy we cannot hear the will of God. We will end up unhappy. To hear anything in our busy and loud culture, we have to find a place where we can hear the will of God. We have to become in sync with the ways of God and the thoughts of God. When that happens, there is peace and harmony with God.

The thing that gives me a wholesome satisfaction and that is preaching and ministry. When I stop, I lose the reason God sent me to earth. During these last days, somebody introduces me and says, "Jim has been preaching for more than 70 years." The audience gasps and often applauds. It was what I was born to do. As long as I have health and I can perform at my level of expectation, I will never quit.

Most people give up too early. Even if they don't die physically, some are dead on the inside. God enables us to not die before we die.

We believe in the historical Jesus. We believe God was living humanly. Early theologians struggled with Jesus being fully divine and yet fully human. The Jesus we meet in the New Testament is an adult.

We can imagine that the public life of Jesus in his second half of life. We meditate on a Jesus ho made friends with every kind of person. Luke's story of the temptations summarizes the encounters of Jesus.

Jesus was led by the Spirit into the desert. Desert is a place of solitude. The desert is where we confront the self. In Christian spirituality, desert is a symbol for retreat and prayer. The result of the struggle is a human that God is pleased with. The desert is the place where we find God.

Jesus went into the desert to pray. He had fasted for 40 days and 40 nights. He was hungry. He was vulnerable. His vision was how things should be in the kingdom of God.

Jesus has power and the source is his Father. The power of a unique person flows from an infinite source that gives enormous potential. Jesus has an immense sense of himself. He always points to the Father as the source. Mark 11:22-23, John 14:5.

Jesus shows us that in every sin there is a potential for good. Love is central to his message. No doubt Jesus was appalled by the contrast between the goodness and love of God which he experienced and the evil and hatred he confronted.

Chapter Eight
Healing

Health is not just the absence of disease. Healing means a new quality of life. Physical conditions have changed from the time life expectancy was merely 40 years. Today some live twice the biblical three score and ten years.

This book is not for only older people living in their final years on earth. If we have not developed self-control by age 30-40, we will not have it. Charles Allen said, "The essence of religion is to adjust the mind and soul. Healing means bringing the person into a right relationship with God into a right relationship with the physical, mental, and spiritual laws of God."

A woman in my pastorate had found in her plight in becoming a widow. In spite of her affliction she appeared to be more youthful. She told me she now had a new problem. She said she had refused the idea of growing old. She was trying to live as if she belonged to a different generation from her own. She dressed young and continued to wear a miniskirt. She wore seductive makeup, youthful clothes, and talked seductively. She was unacceptable of her age. Her behavior was very much like a much younger woman.

Knowing how to grow older is as big a problem for woman who is 20 years old as it is for a 50, 70, or older woman. Older women want to be too active for their age. Some retired from work women son die. Serenity in living never appeared to them.

Setting the life journey and the soul in order is not easy. Love is blind. Fear is even more so. Faith in God can free us. Healing the soul requires a long apprenticeship to mature. All problems in life are linked together. Problems cause reactions. These reactions lead to more problems. Our road to health requires breaking vicious circles. Acceptance of our social condition and becoming sensitive to the reality of our lot in life is the foundation for healing.

We must now live in an atmosphere that is most favorable to health and healing. This does not mean avoiding modes of living but coming into fellowship and intimacy with God at the start and the finishing of our days on earth. The joy of the Lord is our strength necessary for life.

We are not only body and mind, but we are spirit. No physiological or psychological analysis is sufficient to unravel the complexity of living that must be examined before God.

Prayer and meditation enables us to distinguish what things are God-given, and those factors that result from wrong living.

We say that prevention is better than cure. Yet extremely healthy people rarely go for help for living. Younger people do not see the necessity to make themselves healthier and to improve their usefulness to render greater service.

We reach a dead end in human attempts to heal. Some of my difficult patients may come to understand their own mind. They come to realize that they had been distorting their psychological behavior. However, some of this insight was not enough to give them the courage to live and thrive.

When I served as a psychiatric therapist at the Lincoln Regional Center, I saw people who were quite artistic, intuitive, and gentle. They were crushed by the struggle to live. Most were incapable of earning a living in the fast-paced competitive environment. Some were passive but not insensitive. I fund that academically; some patients were brilliant. They are lost and to not make good choices. They share their refuge in their daydreams. They do not have an awareness of God. The administrators of the state hospital tend not to allow the therapists to bring it up.

Healers would profit from a trip to Sant Joseph, Missouri to see the George Glore Psychiatrics Museum to understand what horrid measures were done to attempt to heal people.

John Stott gives us insight on controlling ourselves. He wrote that the crucifixion of the flesh "is something that is not to us, but by us." To take up the cross was Christ's vivid figure of speech for self-denial. Followers of Christ are to behave like condemned prisoners (John Stott, *The Message of Galatians: Only One Way*, p. 113) John 8:31-32.

We react to disappointment the same way as when we were children. The Spirit gives the following transformational truths. I Corinthians 13:11, 14:20. Most self-control issues stem from our immaturity. God can help us develop, perfect, and control our desires, thoughts, and emotions. To be mature, we must put away our childish thinking. In the Greek New Testament, self-control is power over the self or the strength to govern yourself.

In all my years of counseling, my clients been dealing with issues of self-control no matter what their diagnosis says. Self-control regulates one's responses to avoid undesirable behavior. My clients have used many words to describe self-control: determination. Grit. Willpower. Discipline. It is a skill we can learn. An unusual number of youth and adults suffer with attention-deficit disorder with the same obstacles as self-control.

A self-controlled person exhibits strong willpower. They do not act impulsively. They act first without thinking about the consequences. They overreact and experience lasting negative moods.

Some simple interventions include avoiding social media when working so that you do not lose your productivity. Skipping sweet treats to reduce one's sugar intake. Not purchasing something you desire to help stick to a budget. Managing emotion responses when something is done to you that ignites an upset or anger. I find that people of all ages cannot delay gratification. They don't wait to get what they want.

Delaying gratification means to put off short-term desires in favor of long-term rewards. Finding ways to distract ourselves from temptation helps strengthen the ability to delay gratification.

Focusing all our self-control on one obsessive goal makes it difficult to exercise self-control on subsequent tasks throughout the day.

Soul-healing requires a clear goal and motivation to change. Unclear or general goals such as getting stronger leads to failure. Monitoring behavior insures doing the right things that must be done to reach the goal. Find a healthy distraction. Self-control is the most important to improve spiritual, mental, and physical health. We should be reminded of the consequences. These affect our career, finances, relationships, education, self-esteem, and health and well-being.

Self-control is partly influenced by genetics. Life experiences play an important role in strengthening and controlling the ability to control behavior with effort and practice.

Healing comes from learning how to plan effectively. Think through the steps needed to follow including emphasizing long-term goals instead of being persuaded by immediate gratification.

Self-control is power over our will, not only will-power. Proverbs 25:28. We must control our desires and make boundaries to protect our hearts against temptations and attacks. James 1:14-15.

Self-control is produced by the Spirit of God. Fruit grows from branches that are part of the vine. John 15:1-2,5. Jesus is the healing physician so that we can draw from his divine power to produce spiritual fruit in our lives. We will be partakers of Christ's nature. II Peter 1:3-8. It takes self-control to have healing joy when we face difficult situations. I Peter 1:8. Self-control helps us get along with others. We bear the weakness and sins of others rather than condemning them. Self-control helps us to be faithful and not experience fait shattered by the mocking of scoffers. II Peter 3:3-4.

Healing involves keeping track in a journal of the reactions you experienced during the week as demonstrating the fruit of the Spirit. Examine the causes of your reactions.

Find a word, a phrase, or prayer ready in your mind to help you focus on staying in control. Pray God will give you more of the Spirit.

We have never unbreakable steel vessels. We are not independently strong. II Corinthians 4. We were created to be fragile. God allows us to be cracked clay vessels. God places us in situations where we can't make it on the basis of our own strength and wisdom, but on instinct reach out for healing.

Cracked vessels with treasure shining through the cracks is a picture of our being healed. God doesn't always fill our cracks. God uses the cracks to fill us with love, grace, and glory.

God leaves us in a broken world to produce a better way than the comfortable way we are seeking. James 1:2-4. James is not calling for us to know some kind of joyful stoicism. James is writing that the bad things we endure are the tool of a healing God.

Grace comes in uncomfortable forms. As we cry out for healing grace, we are continually receiving it. It is not grace for release. It is the grace we need. Eternal change is what we really need to finish well. II Corinthians 1:3-9.
This fallen world is not our home. I Corinthians 4:16-5;5. This Scripture is about spiritual preparation. This world is not our final destination. We must live in our uncomfortable world of tents and temporary locations. God is preparing us for our eternal home. God gave the Holy Spirit to give us the pass to our heavenly home. There is a home waiting for us where will be warmly welcomed and taken in for eternity.

Healing a soul comes with faith. Faith bridges the awful chasm of unreasonableness. God heals mostly with common sense with reason. All of us trust something. We do not define what is right. God is above us. We are never above God. We are out of control. We do not understand. Proverbs 3:5.

Loving someone deeply is not something we can understand with reason. Relationships are special. And so is our faith.

If I should die tomorrow, I shall be healed of all that ails me. I am ready to go into the arms of a loving God. I have always desired to live a long and healthy life. Everyone dies, but not everyone lives.

Proverbs 13:18. It is important to believe that we are able to grow healthier as we age. Self-control is needed for that.

If we want to slow down our journey in our later years, live a long healthy life, and die suddenly. Eliminate and say no to the things working against you. As we age, our body changes, not just because we are older, but because we do less physically.

People who are healed have heard the message, improved their lifestyles, and now are reaping with joy. They are finishing well. Those who have been healed from self-control gain life satisfaction. They are less prevention-focused on avoiding losses. This shows the futility of working to gain control.

Research defines self-control as "the capacity to alter and regulate response tendencies that result. In the inhibition of undesirable behaviors while promoting desirable actions to support long-time goals. (Tracy Cheung, Marleen Gillebaart, Denise Ridder and others, "Why Are People with High Self-Control Happier," *Personality and Social Psychology*.

Refraining from giving into desires is not the same as striving toward valued goals. Joy comes from actual achievements. During our lifetimes, we encounter differing obstacles in the form of temptations that promise immediate gratification and pleasure that impedes long-term goals.

People who develop self-control are better at managing competing goals by choosing to the goal with more virtuous outcome. They have less motivational conflicts. They are free to pursue their goals. They use their effective imagination and intuition to achieve hopes and aspirations. They ultimately choose joy from the long-term goal despite having to give up on short term gratifications during the times during the goal pursuit.

People enhance their happiness and joy through intentional strategies. They seek personality concordant goals. Self-control is needed for that kind of fruit bearing. Self-control has been linked to success in differing walks of life. With self-control, people focus more on aspirations and less on hinderances. The pursuit of happiness is not easy, but it is within our control.

We are directed to avoid situations that we know where we will encounter temptations. If we are tempted to junk food, we avoid fast-food restaurants. Healing includes avoiding triggers. Strengthening willpower is not easy. It is worth the effort to significantly improve health, work performance, and quality of life. I Corinthians 9:25-26.

When our spirit is nudged by the Spirit, we seek opportunities to make a way for our souls to find Jesus. Ephesians 5:15-18.

We discover in Jesus the secrets to healing. We are guided to grow in being authentic and living into our strengths. We are to go deeper into our relationships. We live in line with our spiritual and ethical ideals. This involves our connections with others. We choose to do what we love to do. And we rejoice in every experience. Joy is our delight when we anticipate, experience, and celebrate things we know are significant. (Pamela E. King, "Joy as a Virtue: The Means and Ends of Joy," *Journal of Psychology and Theology*)

Self-control is one of the important things we need to work on. It must be developed. It has to grow. If we learn to live in the fruit of the Spirit, we will become whole with tremendous peace, ease, and fulfillment.

We will not live in any fruit of the Spirit unless we have self-control. Self-control is required for us to be good, gentle, patient, and to love others. We have to discipline our thoughts. The Holy Spirit will not just zap us with self-control. It is worked out in us.

We learn to have it as our own. We must walk in self-control.

We would be in an irreconcilable mess if God had not equipped us with his wonderful fruit. Matthew 7:15-20. We have the possibility to produce good healthy fruit for others to enjoy. We can help others grow as we and they are transformed by the power of God.

In many churches we often feel that the members are unripe, unhealthy, and spoiled. Unclean and rotten fruit will spoil he entire bunch. It is time we become whole and mature to be healthy, ripe, and nourishing fruit. We can control ourselves if we really want to be healed.

Apply self-control with your thoughts before the hormones rage. Use self-control and get your mind on something else. You do not have to feel like doing it. Do it for your love of God. Choices are made with our self-control.

Spiritual self-control develops an intimate relationship with God. We are refreshed after being in the presence of God. When our mind races into self-pity or anger, we must stop and tell ourselves not to go down that road. This is self-control.

When we travel on the wrong road, we are tired and exhausted. We have to rest from striving so hard. The kingdom of God is within us. What we work so hard for in fact already exists. We apply our self-control to experience the reality of the kingdom. We are called to rejoice. We are called to enjoy all there is. We now have a new attitude toward life. This is found in our inner child. Now that we are traveling on the right road, we are being called to conversion.
The process of conversion calls for continual nourishment of our inner child. Spirituality is our own pattern of life that flows from our personal theology and attitude. Zechariah 8:4-5, 11-12.
God's desire is for us to overcome being offended. This is our enemy's way. Churches of Joy would be healthy if people would use self-control in how they react in the body of Christ.

Control yourself for the love of God. When you love somebody, you want to do what they want you to do. Hebrews 12:11. If you want to have what God wants you to have, you must get into agreement with God. II Corinthians 5:14-15.

From the time I professed faith in Jesus, I have a big collection of Bibles are marked in ink within the words and in the margins of my copies of the Scripture. It is a mystery to somehow I can quickly turn to the words and places where the words are. As a child and youth,

I participated in contests that required quick action to be the first to find a certain Bible verse.

Jesus died so that we no longer have to live selfish and self-centered lives. The love of Christ is our motivator. This helps control us. The more we love God, the more we will be willing to control ourselves.

Our health-care system is not shrinking, but government is expanding its regulatory control. Managing care is the important thing. Cost controls and rationing health services. Health care has come to be "politically correct," or it's just not available.

Paul Tournier is an example of a physician that does not bow to political correctness. He wrote, "I believe that problems can be resolved by grace, like a mist that is dissipated by the sunshine. One sees the Christian gospel of salvation quite concretely at work in the gradual dissolution of tangled problems, without any of them being solved in the usual sense of the word."

All healing people would profit from reading this Swiss doctor's books to gain insights not usually shared. One of the requirements in a nation with strict managed care is the need to be authenticated, documented, effective, relevant, measurable and cost effective. Insurance providers require healers to do more with less. All the reviews methods have been established. Health care is being managed by reviewers outside the clinical setting. To serve in the healing field healers must accept and live with managed care. Neil Anderson, *Christ-Centered Therapy*, pp. 200-275)

The need for healing might be emphasized when a person stumbles and falls. Some people withdraw from an undertaking or project if they accidentally fall when they leave their house. To them, the fall is a bad omen.

Our false step or an awkward movement results from our inattentiveness caused by inner conflict, and from a lack of self-control. This betrays human opposition of the unconscious to he projects of the conscious. This is a representative act of sabotage on the part of our unconsciousness.

An unexpected disappointment in love might be the true cause of taking on a certain vocation. This will result in a bitterness. There often is an inferior complex. A disappointment in love adds to the disquiet set in motion by this and other factors.

Older people must accept a reduction in their expenditure of strength. Rest is needed for their healing, especially during the winter months. Winter holidays may bring more health than those taken in summer.

Finishing well includes a change of habits of the hour we go to bed. Keeping late hours causes a lack of healing that can be cured by the process of re-education.

Our conscious ego serves us well is it is our ego strength that is needed to make concrete in our real-life situation of living, playing, praying and working. As the race of life nears its end, we are called to know experientially that our conscious self is not the consummation of life. We are called to be born again of "water and the Spirit."

Worry, inner and outer conflicts, temptations to impurity, fear, and ambition are causes of unhealthy sleeping habits. Insomnia is not a symptom of sin. It is wrong to suggest that a person who sleeps well is less sinful than those who suffer from insomnia. Some people recover the habit of sleep as a result of transformation of life.

Healing comes as we go to bed in the right state of mind. We become excited by the events of the day. We prolong futile conversations with a friend. We engage in tasks which ought to be fitted into the daytime. We could immerse ourselves in unhealthy reading or other things.

Healing of persons is to not be ashamed of all people, especially children. Jesus knew the needs of our inner child. Mark 10:15. It is the child in us that initiates in us during the second half of life an affirmative and positive attitude toward the aging process. In our old age, the creative, ongoing, and dynamic development goes on in the last seasons of our lives.

I like to do jigsaw puzzles. One night I was possessed by an one-thousand-piece puzzle and before conscious of it, the time quickly jumped to nearly one o'clock in the next morning.

That experience made me more aware that I needed to work harder on my self-control. Life does not have a remote. We must get up and change it ourselves. We had no choice at where we had our beginning.

Beginning well was not my reality. My mother was a 15-year-old girl who rarely went to school. She dropped out in the eighth grade. Her task in her poor family was the care for all the eight children. She washed their clothes on a rub board with bars of lye soap. She did all her duties like a slave. Conversations included shouting, hitting, and silence. She did not know when she was born. She was told it was in her home. That's all.

Lena Mae, my mama, was the oldest, living with her parents squeezed like penned rabbits in their rough-cut shack. Her father had a low-paying job working in a paper mill. It was during the depression, but he was fortunate to have any job. He was often laid off for months. They ate meat-grease gravy, red beans and cornbread, and nobody sat at a table. Each person dipped beans from the pot, flopped cornbread on top, and wandered off to an old dirty floor mattress or a faded sofa found in somebody's trash.

They gathered turnip greens, wild berries, and whatever grew along the roads, eggs from the chickens. They found discarded backbones in trash bins and boiled them with collard greens in a mush.

They moved from Mendota, Virginia to Bristol, Virginia into a place with a dirt floor and chickens running in the house. My mother and father met as he did a paper route to help with his family. Mom was dumpster diving for clothes at Sullins College, where rich college girls pitched clothes. Dad invited her to have an ice cream cone at Anderson Street Park in Bristol. They fell in love. The couple moved into a one-room apartment in downtown Kingsport when they found that she was pregnant to avoid the trauma of relatives and the judging people of Bristol. They married at Broad Street Methodist Church in Kingsport. After I was born, they enrolled me in cradle roll at the First Baptist Church in church square.

When my family moved back to Bristol, they lived above Dink Ameron's grocery store in a one-room apartment on Southside Avenue, across the street from Woodlawn Baptist Church. Church in our culture became all of social life with church activities every day. On Sundays there was Sunday School, then Sunday worship, followed by Baptist Training Union, and evening worship. Monday was for choir practice. Tuesdays for Men's Brotherhood, Royal Ambassadors for boys, Girls Auxiliary, and Women's Missionary Union. Wednesday nights was for choir practice and prayer meetings, Thursdays involved youth groups, churchwide visitation, and cleaning work. Fridays and Saturdays we reached out to nursing homes, jails, so-called shut-ins, and giving food to the poor. Summer camps, Ridgecrest Baptist Assembly, and social events. Eating together as a church family was a big deal. Everybody came and ate. Amazingly, there was always enough for everyone including guests.

Woodlawn held four revivals each year including a youth-led revival. People "got saved" as they "walked the aisles to the front of the church." Revivals were two-weeks long. Each year there was also a two-week Vacation Bible School in which children heard the gospel and Bible stories, made wooden bird houses, and were given the opportunity to trust Jesus as their Savior. They were then baptized into membership in the church. I was baptized at age eight along with many others. Our pastors told us if we were not "saved" or converted by age 12, we probably never would be.

In our two years living in Kingsport, my father made keys and delivered them to people for whom they were made. They had no money for milk. After moving back to Bristol, Dad found a job at Barr's Sporting Goods. He worked for Edward and Herb Barr for many years. He made $37.50 per week.

My youngest brother David wrote a huge book tracing details of generations back to Robert II, "Robert the Bruce," in Scotland. Amazing book. David spent years in research and gave copies of the cherished work to others and myself.

The book represents what we can be when we have to be. We can do more than we can imagine when life requires it.

I was the first person in my family, on both mom and dad's sides, to graduate from high school. My grandfather walked from his home on the Virginia side of Bristol to see me graduate from Tennessee High School in Bristol.

Mom prayed that I would serve as a preacher. She wanted Ed and David to also amount to something. After high school, I saved my money from delivering the *Bristol Herald Courier* and mowing yards. I worked in the college cafeteria at Carson-Newman College for sixty cents an hour to pay the tuition and costs. I could never do that today. Tuition and books were low, not the huge costs that families have to pay with huge student loans. Only athletes go to school without paying, but they are paid to be in school. Before the age of big-time sports, student athletes were composed of whoever was in the school. They had no special tutors. They ate the same meals as everybody else.

Most of the coaches were the teachers, who coached sports without any extra pay. Small colleges played large universities. The University of Tennessee played Carson-Newman, King, Tusculum, Emory and Henry, Maryville, and other small schools.

Most religious colleges held daily chapel meetings with required attendance. Carson-Newman held morning watch and vespers as additional times for worship.

College transfigured me. When someone comes looking for the old you, pulling old triggers, but cannot find the person who began life as you did, that is healing.

The magic miracle lies in honoring our journey and being rooted in who and where we are today.

I want to finishing the race of life well. I want to be filled with hope, looking forward to tomorrow, not just waiting for the end of my life.

Life is meant to be lived.

Ending well requires us to surrender to people we want to be with, with people who embrace us and make us feel loved and wanted.

As I grow older, positivity is not the key to survival. The key is acceptance and gratitude. We accept the good and bad days. Accepting brings eternal joy and peace. Making a change in life is difficult.

God keeps an eye on us all the time. We can chose to do miracles in our lives. We are actors in a play. We are writers of our own story. We are not serving a death sentence.

God knows the details of our lives. Scripture gives us the insight that our Creator knew and loved us from our beginning to our finishing.

Our finishing may come by natural means, by our being killed in war or on the street, by cancer and innumerable diseases, in an automobile or boat or farm machine accident, in fire or flood, by hunger from lack of food or water.

Just five decades ago, a United States bomber broke apart over North Carolina. The crash dropped a payload of two 3.8-megaton hydrogen bombs. Each bomb had sufficient explosive power to be 300 times the power of the bomb that landed on Hiroshima at the ending of World War II.

One bomb had a parachute deploy and landed nose down in a field standing straight up. The other parachute did not deploy. They couldn't find it.

The recently declassified account of the event now fifty years old, told that Lt. Jack Revelle was given a ten-man crew to find it. For many days they dug into the swamp searching for the bomb. If they had failed, there would have been no life or future.

The configuration of the United States would become forever changed. Radiation would have traveled through to New York and beyond. Finding the bombs had eternal consequences.

Today's bombs are more powerful than we could ever imagine. Some mad, insane dictator could drop a bomb that would destroy the earth and all life.

Without self-control, we would have absolutely no control over how life would end.

Finishing well requires that we take what life hands us and make more of it than the culture expects. What gets in the way of finishing well? We say when circumstances do not go our way. How we choose to deal with adversity reveals more about us than our blessings.

I have learned about things that have impeded living my best life by learning about my ancestors. We make decisions that do not serve us in the long term.

Our belief systems stop us. We say, "I can't." Or "that's impossible." We long for things we don't have, rather than loving the things we do not have. We must value the people in our lives who brings us joy. That is the pathway to satisfying lives and gratitude. Surrounding ourselves with the things and people who replenish and support us on our journey is to finish our race well.

Bibliography

Arndt, William, Frederick W. Danker, Walter Bauer, and Franklin Wilbur Gingrich. *A Greek-English Lexicon of the New Testament and Other Early Christian Literature*. Chicago: University of Chicago Press, 2002.

Anderson, Neil T., Terry Zuchlike, and Julianne Zuchlike. *Christ-Centered Therapy: The Practical Integration of Theology and Psychology*. Grand Rapids, Michigan: Zondervan Publishing House, 2020.

Bakke, Dennis W. *Joy at Work: A Revolutionary Approach to Fun on the Job*. New York: Pear Press, 2006.

Bass, Diane Butler. *Perceiving Possibilities*. Topeka, Kansas: Great Plains Conference of the United Methodist Church, 2024.

Baumeister, Robert F. "Ego-Depletion: Is the Active Self a Limited Resource?" *Journal of Personality and Social Psychology*, 1998.

Blanchard, Kenneth. *We Are the Beloved: A Spiritual Journey*. Grand Rapids, Michigan: Zondervan, 1994.

Cheung, Tracy, Marleen Gillebart, and Denise Ridder. "Why Are People with High Self-Control Happier?" *Personality and Social Psychology*, Volume 5, July 8, 2024.

Cox, Harvey. *Feast of Fools*. Cambridge, Massachusetts: Harvard University Press, 1969.

Gray, Donald P. "Prayer: Passing Over and Coming Back," *Worship*, Volume 48, Number 5, pp. 300-301, May 1974.

Hewitt, Arthur Wentworth. *Highland Shepherds*. San Francisco; Harper and Row, 1955.

Hillman, James. *Blue Fire*. New York: Harper and Row, 1991.

Joy, Donald. *Bonding: Relationships in the Image of God.* Dalles: Word Books, 1999.

Kierkegaard, Soren. *The Journals,* translated and edited by Alexander Dru, London: Oxford University Press, p. 15, August 1835, published 1938.

Killinger, John. "The Overflowing Cup," in *Pulpit Digest,* March-April 1992, pp. 13-17.

King, Pamela E., "Joy as a Virtue: The Means and Ends of Joy," *Journal of Psychology and Theology, 2020.*

McReynolds, David. *The Genealogical History of Our Family,* Self-published, Knoxville, Tennessee, 2019.

McReynolds, James E. *Alcohol: America's Number One Drug Problem.* Nashville: Broadman Press, 1977.

McReynolds, James E. *Joy Beyond the Walls of This World: Healing the Souls of Men . . . and Women.* Cleveland, Tennessee: Parson's Porch Books, 2021.

McReynolds, James E., "Long Distant Parenting and Self-Control," *Christian Single Magazine,* January 1990, pp. 36-37.

McReynolds, James E. *The Joy of Prayer as Intimacy with God.* Cleveland, Tennessee: Parson's Porch Books, 2021.

McReynolds, *The Theological Mystery of the Anabaptists.* Elkhart, Indiana: Anabaptist Books, 1970.

Mooney, A.J. and Arlene and Howard Eisenberg. *The Recovery Book.* New York: Workman Publishing Company, 1992.

Murphy, Joseph. *The Power of Your Subconscious Mind.* New York: Bantom Books, 1982.

O'Neal, John R. *The Paradox of Success: When Winning at work Means*

Losing at Life: A Book of Renewal for Leaders. New York: G. P. Putnam Books, 1993.

Stott, John. *The Message of Galatians: Only One Way.*Downers Grove, Illinois: InterVarsity Press, 1986.

Sheehy, Gail. *New Passages: Making Your Life Across Time.* Thorndike, Maine: G. K. Hall and Company, 1997.

Thomas, Ernest. *The Power of Prayer.* Nashville: Discipleship Resources-Tidings, 1975.

Tillich, Paul. *The Courage to Be.* New Haven: Yale University Press, 1952.

Tournier, Paul. *A Place for You.* Evanston, Illinois: Harper and Row, 1968.

Willard, Dallas. *The Spirit of the Disciplines: Understanding How God Changes Lives.* San Francisco: Harper and Row, 1990.

Zukav, Gary. *The Seat of the Soul.* New York: Fireside Books and Simon and Schuster, 1990.

About the Author

Words for the tombstone of Jim McReynolds: Minister of Joy to the World. He has served more than 70 years in dedicated ministries, enabling his leadership to be extended globally during his earthly journey.

Jim continues to inspire through writing books and articles. He lives with his wife Laurel in a new home in Elmwood, Nebraska. Gratitude is the tailwind that enables them to travel farther with a joyous spirit. They have their low times, but with resilience, they bounce back.

He is a natural therapist who served as a psychiatric therapist II for the Lincoln Regional Center that houses most severe mental health problems. Jim earned the doctor of psychology degree from Christ Church College of the University of Oxford with intern work at the Appalachian Counseling Center in Bristol, Tennessee.

Dr. John R. Killinger has been Jim's best friend and mentor for more than 50 years. Killinger was a professor at Vanderbilt University Divinity School, where Jim earned his master of divinity and doctor of divinity degrees.

Many of the forewords to Jim's books were written by Killinger. These forewords have been essential for readers to gain insight into the joy of the Lord. Readers finally arrive at discovering the link between the joy of God and the glory of God. Both Killinger and McReynolds enable the world to see this radiation of joy from the love and grace of God.

Both writers and preachers expressed the knack of living with an attitude of gratitude. They are now retired stopping for a rest. Pausing to really see the world. John is in his 90s, Jim his 80's. They make interludes of thankfulness to keep the energy going despite the pains of old age.